GARY THOMAS

AND DRS. STEVE & REBECCA WILKE

9

MUST-HAVE

CONVERSATIONS

FOR A DOUBT-FREE

WEDDING DAY

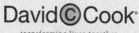

David C Cook®

transforming lives together

9 MUST-HAVE CONVERSATIONS FOR A DOUBT-FREE WEDDING DAY
Published by David C Cook
4050 Lee Vance Drive
Colorado Springs, CO 80918 U.S.A.

David C Cook U.K., Kingsway Communications
Eastbourne, East Sussex BN23 6NT, England

The graphic circle C logo is a registered trademark of David C Cook.

The website addresses recommended throughout this book are offered as a
resource to you. These websites are not intended in any way to be or imply an
endorsement on the part of David C Cook, nor do we vouch for their content.

All Scripture quotations, unless otherwise marked, are taken from the Holy
Bible, New International Version®, NIV®. Copyright © 1973, 1984 by Biblica,
Inc.™ Used by permission of Zondervan. All rights reserved worldwide.
www.zondervan.com. Scripture quotations marked NRSV are taken from
the New Revised Standard Version Bible, copyright 1989, Division of
Christian Education of the National Council of the Churches of Christ in
the United States of America. Used by permission. All rights reserved.
The author has added italics to Scripture quotations for emphasis.

LCCN 2012951905
ISBN 978-1-4347-0549-5
eISBN 978-0-7814-0876-9

© 2013 Gary Thomas, Steve Wilke, and Rebecca Wilke
Published in associations with Yates & Yates, www.yates2.com.
Previously published as The Sacred Search Couple's Conversation Guide

The Team: Alex Field, Karen Lee-Thorp, Amy Konyndyk,
Nick Lee, Caitlyn Carlson, Karen Athen
Cover Design: JWH Graphic Arts, James Hall

Printed in the United States of America
First Edition 2013

7 8 9 10 11 12 13 14 15 16

062117

CONTENTS

AUTHORS' NOTE   5

FOR PASTORS   7

FOR COUPLES: HOW TO USE THIS CONVERSATION GUIDE   11

SESSION 1: PRE-ENGAGEMENT PUNCH LIST   17

SESSION 2: THE DOUBT-FREE WEDDING DAY   25

  DEVOTIONAL: TWO ARE BETTER THAN ONE   35

SESSION 3: YOUR COVENANT MARRIAGE   39

  DEVOTIONAL: *DIVORCE* DIVORCE   47

SESSION 4: AND THE TWO SHALL BECOME ONE   51

  DEVOTIONAL: MOVING TOWARD EACH OTHER   59

SESSION 5: BUILDING A FAMILY   63

  DEVOTIONAL: SOMEDAY   71

SESSION 6: CONSTRUCTIVE CONFLICT   75

  DEVOTIONAL: VACATION VANITY   85

SESSION 7: DEVELOPING AND MAINTAINING SEXUAL INTIMACY   89

  DEVOTIONAL: THE POWER OF A PURE PASSION   99

SESSION 8: MONEY, MONEY, MONEY   103

  DEVOTIONAL: FINANCES   111

SESSION 9: SPIRITUAL INTIMACY   113

  DEVOTIONAL: "POWER" COUPLES   119

APPENDIX A: THE MARRIAGE MENTOR'S
              CONVERSATIONAL SESSION GUIDE   123

APPENDIX B: PERSONAL HISTORY QUESTIONNAIRE   139

AUTHORS' NOTE

This conversation guide is intended for use between couples and marriage mentors. It is not intended to replace the psychological or medical care of a professional, licensed provider. We estimate that 50 percent of couples may need professional care related to one or more issues in our guide, so the best marriage mentors will have a resource list available for qualified referrals to such providers.

Such issues will typically be identified when the Personal History Questionnaire is filled out (see Appendix B) or at any time in the conversations when the couple is not able to discuss and agree on one or more topics. If concerns arise at any point in this process, a referral should be made to supplement these conversations and marriage mentoring. At that time, the marriage mentor should obtain a "release of information" from the professional provider in order to talk openly about the counseling process and to hold the couple accountable as they prepare for marriage.

FOR PASTORS

The vast majority of couples considering marriage will walk into *your* office, not the office of a licensed professional marriage counselor. And if you're like most pastors, you're probably already overwhelmed with the process of running a church, so you may feel unsure about how to implement the nine sessions included in this book. Don't worry! This conversation guide is not here to add stress to your ministry. Instead, our plan is to help you in the extremely important process of preparing couples for the commitment of sacred marriage. Here are some initial thoughts to assist you:

1. Premarital counseling may be one of the most important responsibilities you and your staff address. You are preparing a man and woman to become a couple and probably soon to become a family.

2. We have worked with hundreds of struggling married couples over the years, and we're convinced that a process like this *before marriage*

would keep half of them out of our counseling office and even more out of the divorce courts. Imagine that—you, your pastoral staff, and lay leaders who help as marriage mentors could directly affect the divorce rate of your church and community.

3. Marriage mentoring doesn't have to rest on your shoulders alone. However, since you or one of your pastoral staff will actually sign the marriage certificate, you should be able to "sign off" on the couple's readiness for marriage with complete confidence. In other words, it is up to the pastor to assure that the couple has taken time to carefully go through all nine sessions with each other and a marriage mentor.

4. The position of marriage mentor could be assigned to an elder or other mature member of your church family. The mentor can be an individual or a married couple. The qualities you should look for in mentors are wisdom; confidentiality; a strong track record in their own marriage; good people skills; the ability to listen to others rather than preach at them; and the ability to discuss a couple's personal issues forthrightly, maturely, with tact, and without embarrassment.

5. Some couples may choose to have someone outside of your church serve as a marriage mentor. That person doesn't need professional counseling qualifications, because this conversation guide provides them with the tools they need for in-depth discussions with those who are considering marriage.

6. If a couple has issues the marriage mentor isn't equipped to handle, he or she should refer that couple to a professional counselor. If your church doesn't have a list of qualified, licensed counseling or mental-health providers in your area, now would be an excellent time to research those resources.

This conversation guide invites a pre-marriage couple into a deep and time-intensive process. We encourage you to implement this guide in a way that has satisfying results for everyone involved. Some couples may tell you they don't need or want this, but you have probably seen your share of married couples in trouble. This premarital process is not a chat—it's a conversation that will take time. In the long run, however, it will help couples avoid problems and improve satisfaction as their marriage progresses. So give this pre-marriage couple the gift of strongly advising them to embrace this conversation guide for their benefit now and in their future. We pray that this conversation will be a blessing to you and your ministry.

FOR COUPLES

How to Use This Conversation Guide

The pastor looked at the couple in front of him with concern. He knew they were both young, still in college, and bringing baggage from both of their families of origin that could cause any number of significant marital problems for years to come. Yet they proclaimed themselves "deeply in love," and because they were Christians, they said they believed marriage was the right next step for them.

The pastor couldn't shake his concerns. He realized he should do something, but what? After going through some of his notes for the premarital counseling session, he decided to ask the young man to step out of the room for a few minutes. Then he turned to the woman and asked, "Are you *sure* you want to do this?"

She stared at him in surprise, uncertain she'd heard him correctly. She finally replied, "Excuse me, pastor. What do you mean?"

"I'm just wondering if you're sure you know what you are getting into. Do you really want to get married right now?"

"Oh yes, of course I do!" She nodded to emphasize the point.

The pastor called her fiancé back into the room and, despite his doubts, moved on with the counseling session and eventually the wedding.

In hindsight, what that pastor should have done was directly share his concerns with the couple—together. He should have said something like: "You two aren't ready to get married. I have some serious doubts about you and your marriage if you continue on this path. In fact, I have lots of doubts!" But he was too kindhearted and perhaps a little naive and uncertain about how to counsel a couple who really needed to take more time before they walked down the aisle.

As for the couple, they certainly could have used much more than one session of required premarital counseling, because the pastor was correct—they weren't as prepared as they should have been. They *weren't* ready to get married. Not only were they young, but they also hadn't addressed some of the most important matters couples should discuss long before they even get engaged, let alone go through premarital counseling.

And yet, by God's grace, this couple survived. Actually, they've done much more than that: they recently celebrated their thirty-year wedding anniversary, launched two great sons into adulthood, and for decades have counseled on these very issues around marriage, family, and parenting. How do we know? Because Steve and Rebecca are this formerly underprepared couple!

Yes, Steve and Rebecca survived—but how much better it would have been for them if they could have *thrived* during those early years of marriage. The three of us (throwing Gary in here now) have seen firsthand how many of the struggles that married couples experience can be avoided, or at least minimized, if men and women would have serious and substantial conversations, just like those included in this guide, prior to getting married. (It would be even better to have these conversations prior to getting *engaged*.) Every couple—whether just considering marriage, planning a wedding, or even journeying through marriage—should be sure they've taken time to talk over the specific critical questions covered in each of the sessions that follow. Your authors have witnessed how these conversations prepare couples for the challenges ahead of them, and this couple's conversation guide is designed to set you up for the best marriage possible.

It may feel like a lot of work, and you probably *will* feel uncomfortable at times. In the end, however, going through these sometimes-painful issues will save you from more hurtful work or even catastrophe, so take your time and get ready to approach your wedding day with renewed confidence based upon wise preparation.

GUIDELINES FOR GETTING THE MOST OUT OF THIS GUIDE

We're going to spend nine weeks (or nine sessions) to prepare you for what will be a major event—a couple celebrating the beautiful commitment of marriage with friends and family. The first few sessions might scare you a bit. *9 Must-Have Conversations for a Doubt-Free Wedding Day* seeks to get you to look into the rearview mirror at any past baggage or burdens that might take away from or erode the passion, romance, and intimacy of your marriage, so expect us to probe a little bit—and even to raise some questions that boldly ask, "Are you sure about your decision to marry the person you're having this conversation with?" If your match is wise, this will simply confirm the choice you're making. If it's less than wise, or premature, it's an act of love for someone to point that out.

Sorting through these issues and knowing *why* you're choosing to marry this person is a necessary step to becoming one flesh before God and to fortifying yourself against the inevitable doubts that will certainly follow in your future together. You can look at this time not only as a preparation for marriage but as the first steps for the two of you to actually begin merging two lives into one.

Each session has detailed content for you to review, work through, and discuss together. We have developed this content over many decades in both field and clinical experiences. Each session also includes a series of questions to answer—first personally, then discussed as a couple with your mentor, who can assist you through this process. We have included additional topics and questions that your mentor should use in this conversation process. Appendix A provides the Marriage Mentor's Conversational Session Guide.

We suggest the following guidelines for the two of you to agree to follow before you start the upcoming sessions and conversations.

- **Keep an open mind.** Both of you need to have an open mind to the (1) content, (2) conversations, and (3) outcome of these conversations. By doing so, you will have the greatest potential for success, both now and in your future.
- **Hold nothing back.** This process is not the time to fearfully avoid hard truth and painful revelations, be politically correct, or shade your answers

to keep from potentially hurting yourself or your future mate. By being honest, transparent, and vulnerable about absolutely everything (past and present), the two of you will know each other better than before and feel confident about your potential as a couple and about one of the most important decisions in your lives. Any part of this conversation you choose to avoid is likely the most important part of your history that needs to be processed with your partner and mentor. We have found that personal edits (questions and topics you want to avoid) are the exact issues that have the greatest potential to doom marriages and families down the road. Our offices are full of couples who avoided facing the hard issues, *but that didn't make the issues go away—it just left the couple unprepared to face them.*

- **Don't fear the outcome.** Nothing productive can take place if you are fearful about the outcome of this conversation. Trust this time-tested process. It has worked for countless couples before you.

- **Find a qualified marriage mentor.** We strongly recommend that you find a qualified individual(s) to assist you as you work through these sessions. This can be a mentor, pastor, or professional counselor. Often couples can be blind to critical issues that arise, but an objective, seasoned marriage professional will pick up on vital issues and also point out areas of concern that you or your potential spouse might otherwise miss. Our experience is that those of you who try this on your own do so for reasons that will hurt, not help, your relationship and marriage.

- **Read, write, and then discuss.** These sessions and their conversations have been designed in a strategic manner that will work best when you individually read through the content, write down your own answers privately, and then meet with your potential mate and your mentor to share your answers and spend time delving deeper into conversations about the content. Sometimes people try to renegotiate these three steps—for example, talking through the questions together without writing anything down. Optimal results will only be obtained when you follow the "read, write, and then discuss" method we have scripted here for you.

After many of the sessions you will find a devotional—a few pages of text that take the topic of that session a bit further. If possible, read this material when you finish writing your answers for that session.

PRE-ENGAGEMENT PUNCH LIST

Falling in love with someone and finding out they want to spend the rest of their life with you is one of the most exhilarating of all human experiences. In fact, the emotions are hard to describe to someone who hasn't experienced this stage of love for themselves. We just can't believe anyone else has ever felt quite the way we do.

Ironically, this passionate wave of emotion is exactly what complicates the next important stages of relational development that eventually lead to a marital covenant. The overwhelming ecstasy of this season of courtship masks some critical matters that need to be addressed well before an actual engagement occurs and certainly long before the wedding is planned and takes place.

Unfortunately, most of the couples we talk to have rarely taken the time or made the preparatory effort to discuss the crucial topics essential for a successful marriage. Sadly, little or minimally effective counseling occurs once the date has been set and the honeymoon has been booked. Couples are focused on choosing the right dress and tux, picking out the most beautiful flowers, and choosing the decorations, all but ignoring the preparation necessary to get your heart, soul, mind, and body ready to enter marriage.

In our experience, the very topics that should be covered pre-engagement, or certainly pre-marriage, are the same subjects that routinely show up in marriage counseling offices somewhere down the road. *That's* why we feel so strongly about these conversations taking place early and often in your courtship. Premarital counseling must include the content and questions that we have provided here for you.

We'll be honest—throughout our writing of this guide, birthed in prayer and dialogue with each other, was this central aim: how do we keep more couples out of our offices because their marriage is making them miserable, and in their homes and communities where they can passionately love each other and pursue God's purpose for their lives?

At the outset, there are six items on our Pre-engagement Punch List we'd like you both to review. Just as a contractor would compile a punch list to ensure the success of a project, we're recommending that you take time to analyze these prerequisites prior to completing the sessions ahead of you:

1. **Start pre-engagement conversations.** If you haven't already begun having these kinds of conversations, it's vital that you start now. If nothing else, getting in the practice of talking in depth about significant relational topics will be excellent practice for the two of you to begin building relational intimacy.

2. **Avoid unrealistic expectations.** Each of you needs to be honest about the balance of reality versus fantasy. Depending upon who you are and where you have been (your personal stories and histories), each of you will have your own expectations about what love, romance, and marriage will look like. Adopting unrealistic expectations for each other is one of the biggest mistakes couples make—whether they are dating, engaged, or married.

3. **Realize that pain and suffering are guaranteed and a significant part of our lives.** Life this side of heaven is never going to be perfect, and pain is part of the human experience. Problems—including some really big ones—are guaranteed. This is why wedding vows often include the phrase "for better or worse." Yes, there will be plenty of seasons filled with sunshine and bliss, but there will also be bleaker days with sorrow and suffering. Marriage is about helping each other through life's entire journey.

4. **Accept the flawed sinner.** No matter whom you date and eventually marry, everyone is a flawed sinner—beginning with you. Accepting this fact about each other not only helps alleviate unrealistic expectations, but it should also prompt

both of you to develop your spiritual walk with the Lord. Only with His divine assistance will we be able to work on our flaws and become the best we can be for Him and each other. Gary's book *Sacred Marriage* made its mark with this provocative question: "What if God designed marriage to make us holy more than to make us happy?" Few people think of marriage this way going *in*, but most married couples eventually find it to be all too true.

5. **Be aware of baggage, burdens, and blessings.** In addition to your flawed sin nature, each of you will bring an assortment of baggage, burdens, and blessings into your relationship. Embrace this reality now, but also take time in pre-engagement or pre-marriage conversations to understand the balance of baggage and burdens versus blessings. Each will have an impact on you both, as well as everyone you love and everyone who loves you. That's a huge responsibility, so buyer beware: if either of you is overwhelmed with the baggage, then take the necessary time to work through those issues before you exchange wedding vows. You are not morally obligated to accept anyone's baggage prior to marriage, but once the vows are given and the rings are exchanged, your spouse's baggage becomes your own—all of it!

6. Recognize that contempt is never acceptable.
Yes, we're asking you to evaluate each other, but disrespect and contempt are unhealthy in any relationship, especially in the most intimate one between a husband and wife. Over time, these feelings will erode what was once lovely and beautiful. Marital conflict is unavoidable, so you both must learn to resolve conflict respectfully. Once we see contempt in couples, we know the prognosis is poor. A good counselor won't just look at *what* you say when you answer these questions, but also the *way* you say it, the way you look at each other, the way you treat each other, the way you speak of and to each other.

As you work through this punch list, think about yourself first and then your partner. Is there an area(s) of concern that you can identify already? If so, take time now to think it through more deeply. After you've done that, consider the following questions.

1. What attracted you to each other?

2. Share one or more unrealistic, ridiculous, silly expectation you have about your partner.

3. Make a list of three things you absolutely will never tolerate from your future mate.

4. Will you view "for better, for worse—in sickness and in health" as a reality for your future? What exceptions do you have to this perspective on marriage?

5. How well do you understand your potential mate's family and personal history? Have you discussed family relationships, previous marriages, and medical/psychological issues in extended family members? What questions and concerns do you still have?

6. How would you describe your potential mate's daily walk with God?

7. How would you describe their relationship strengths and weaknesses? Make a list of at least three strengths and three weaknesses that you can share with each other.

More than anything, this session has raised *questions* rather than provided any answers, but the process will give your mentor a chance to get to know where you are as a couple and will help you know what still needs to be explored in your relationship. Now, take a break, go have some fun times together, but get ready to get serious again in session 2 as we prepare you for a Doubt-Free Wedding Day.

THE DOUBT-FREE WEDDING DAY

Every wedding day is different, and every individual faces it with fears, delusions, fantasies, doubts, excitement, joy, laughter, and even tears. Our hope for you is that you will have a fantastic and exciting wedding day, with the confidence that comes from knowing you have prepared for this special day as much as any couple could. The best way to achieve this is to do your premarital homework and work through any potential problems or doubts ahead of time. In doing this, you're going beyond simply making a wise decision; you're also setting the foundation from which you can tackle any future issues that will arise along the way.

For the most part, this session isn't a test with right or wrong answers. Be honest, open, and vulnerable as you answer each question. This will help the two of you understand each other and your growing identity as a couple. It will only be as effective, however, as your *honesty* and *courage*. If you deliberately shade the truth because you want to avoid hurting your future spouse or perhaps are afraid of raising uncomfortable issues, or if you hold back on your answers and the dialogue that follows, that lack of courage and honesty will send your relationship down an unhealthy path before your marriage even begins.

Many times in Scripture, before God did something *really big*, He prefaced His instructions with these words: "Don't be afraid."

- That night the LORD appeared to [Isaac] and said, "I am the God of your father Abraham. Do not be afraid." (Gen. 26:24)
- Then the LORD said to Joshua, "Do not be afraid." (Josh. 8:1)
- But the LORD said to [Gideon], "Peace! Do not be afraid." (Judg. 6:23)
- The angel of the LORD said to Elijah, "… Do not be afraid." (2 Kings 1:15)
- But the LORD said to me [Jeremiah], "… Do not be afraid." (Jer. 1:7–8)
- "And you, [Ezekiel], do not be afraid of them or their words. Do not be afraid, though briers and thorns are all around you and you live among scorpions." (Ezek. 2:6)
- "Do not be afraid, Daniel. Since the first day that you set your mind to gain understanding and to humble yourself before your God, your words were heard, and I have come in response to them." (Dan. 10:12)
- But Jesus immediately said to them: "Take courage! It is I. Don't be afraid." (Matt. 14:27)

- The angel said to the women, "Do not be afraid." (Matt. 28:5)
- One night the Lord spoke to Paul in a vision: "Do not be afraid." (Acts 18:9)
- Then he placed his right hand on me [John] and said: "Do not be afraid. I am the First and the Last." (Rev. 1:17)

Preparing for marriage and family is one of those really big decisions that takes courage. So with these verses in mind, ask God to assist you in completing this conversation guide with integrity, honesty, and courage. In this exercise, the biblical truth that we will reap what we sow is particularly true.

Don't worry. No couple is perfectly matched. Human clones don't exist, and if they did, they wouldn't get married. That's why in *The Sacred Search* there's a chapter entitled, "You're Looking for a Complement, Not a Clone." You can read more about this there. Here we want to help you find out where you disagree with each other, as well as any potential roadblocks to intimacy. And that's what you want, right? To really know each other and to be known? To grow together so that your future spouse becomes and remains your best friend? Here's your chance to start building such a relationship right now.

REASONS AND QUESTIONS

1. Write down the three best reasons you're getting married *to this particular person*. Your list does not have to be in any particular order, but it

should include the top three most significant reasons you want to marry your fiancé/fiancée. Feel free to list more, but write at least three.

2. The next question will be a bit more difficult, but it's just as important as the first one. If someone thought you were acting too hastily or that you were choosing poorly, what would they say makes your choice to get married a questionable one? This doesn't mean you agree with it, but try to be objective. What objections might someone raise (or what objections have others already raised) about why the two of you shouldn't get married right now, or why you should be concerned about marrying the person that you've chosen? Write down at least three.

Discuss these questions and answers with your marital conversation facilitator. Spend some time praying through these possible objections. Ask God to open you up to His conviction or confirmation. If any one answer causes you to be uneasy or uncomfortable, we encourage you to dig a little deeper with your mentor. Remember, we can help you locate the red flags, but we can't resolve them. That's something you have to take responsibility for.

For the questions that follow, don't skip those that scare you. In fact, we request that you spend most of your conversation on the areas that are *most* uncomfortable. We like to say that you need to get comfortable learning to scuba dive, not just snorkel, at this stage in your relationship. Snorkeling—staying on the surface—is fine for a couple who are simply dating. When you're talking marriage, you've got to get below the surface and find out what's going on in the depths of that person's heart and soul.

It will be a tremendous gift on your wedding day to know that you have prayed and thought through every potential objection. It's normal to feel a little overwhelmed and scared at the thought of committing your life to someone. Having prayed through it thoroughly and talked through it completely with your marriage mentor will help you overcome any significant wedding-day doubts and will lead you to a day of confident joy.

3. What current doubts do you have about the wisdom of getting married to your partner at this particular moment? Are there any questions you need to seek answers to before making such a major commitment?

4. Have you spoken to anyone about these doubts? Have you discussed them together? Will you do so now?

WHAT DO YOU MEAN?

If I tell you I'm going to exercise, you don't really know what I mean, do you? I could be planning on going for a run, playing volleyball or basketball, lifting weights, going to a spinning class, joining a soccer game, or working out on an elliptical machine. *Exercise* is a generic word with many specific meanings. A guy pumping iron and a woman running a half marathon are both exercising, but they're also doing two very different things—which means that if I tell you I enjoy exercising, you don't really know if you'd enjoy exercising *with me*, because there are so many different ways to exercise.

The same is true of the word *marriage*. When you think about what it means to get married, you have a picture in your mind of what a marriage relationship looks like, but that picture may be very different from what your potential spouse thinks marriage looks like. You're both talking about "being married," but one person may be imagining a very different kind of relationship. In this section, we're going to help the two of you get on the same page.

It will be most helpful for you if you've already read the chapter in *The Sacred Search* entitled "What's Your Style?" (chapter 9) before completing these questions.

5. Describe your parents' marriage in a few sentences. What did it look like when you were growing up? What were their strengths? Their weaknesses?

6. In what ways would you like your own marriage to resemble your parents' marriage?

7. In what ways would you like your own marriage to be different from your parents' marriage?

8. Which one of the marriage styles listed in chapter 9 of *The Sacred Search* most closely resembles the vision of marriage you've grown up with?

9. Which style of marriage would be most difficult for you to be part of?

10. Given your preferred style, write down three things that you think make your fiancé/fiancée a particularly wise choice for you.

11. This one will be more difficult to answer. Remember, there are no perfect spouses out there. Every couple will have something to work on for as long as their relationship lasts. Admitting some weaknesses won't doom your relationship; it simply points out what you need to work on. List two of the biggest fears you have for a marriage to the person you're currently engaged to.

12. Are there any other questions or concerns that you have about your partner and this marriage that haven't been shared up to this point?

Okay, we've contemplated a number of important issues you will face as a married couple. Good work. Now keep moving forward. Continue working through these conversational areas with counsel to determine if they rise above the level of "normal differences" to "dangerously incompatible." Writing and talking about these life-changing issues face-to-face with qualified counsel makes the truth become far more apparent. Either you will see the realities and challenges more clearly, or you might have your fears melt away. Relational and marital conflict is a normal and ongoing part of married life. If you run from these issues, you're not ready to be married. However, if you know that you've done your homework by prayerfully facing these issues in an honest and forthright manner, you can quiet your fears and focus on the joy and wonder of committing your heart to the love of your life.

TWO ARE BETTER THAN ONE[1]

Gary warned Malcolm[2] to think twice—and maybe three times—before he married Laura. Several of Malcolm's friends had as well. Malcolm and his girlfriend fought all the time when they were dating, in part because they were on opposite ends of the spectrum. Malcolm could be harsh and blunt. His girlfriend, Laura, was very sensitive. On one occasion, Malcolm "confronted" Laura with seven ways she was failing as a girlfriend. When Gary expressed his incredulity that Malcolm could dump so much on her at one time, Malcolm responded, "But Gary, I could have said so much more!"

And yet, as Malcolm and Laura pursued Christ, they both grew in many positive ways. Malcolm might have grown up without tact,

---

1 Several of the ending devotionals in this conversation guide are based on teachings and anecdotes included in some of Gary's other books, including *Sacred Marriage*, *Devotions for a Sacred Marriage*, *Devotions for Sacred Parenting*, and *Holy Available*.

2 Not his real name.

but to his credit he began practicing the Christian virtue of humility, willingly schooling himself on Laura's sensitivity. Laura respected Malcolm's courage to tell the truth, regardless of the consequences, and realized that always being soft wasn't the loving response in every circumstance. Over two decades later, they have a marvelous relationship and a beautiful, God-honoring marriage. Each one has helped the other draw closer to God in character, as each one represented (almost to an extreme) God's strength and God's tenderness.

You don't need to find someone like you, but you *do* need to find someone you like, someone you respect, someone who inspires you. While people who surrender to Christ and open themselves up to the Holy Spirit's work can and do evolve, we don't, in a *personality* sense, become completely different people. Malcolm can still be blunt; Laura is still sensitive. But they like and respect that about each other. If Malcolm looked down on sensitive people, he wouldn't have any respect for Laura, and he'd start treating her in a condescending way, and their marriage would suffer.

If you have real problems with your fiancé/fiancée's personality now, marriage will likely increase those problems, not solve them. Keep in mind that someone to whom you'd have a very difficult time being married could be an ideal partner for someone else. You're not judging a person's character, you're simply exploring your compatibility as a married couple—which is why these questions are designed to help you understand this person and thoughtfully consider what it will be like for *you* (not anyone else) to be married to this person.

Don't make the mistake many do and fall for a person's *potential*. You'll ruin this exercise if you think you can substantially change the person you're marrying. It's a mistake to marry someone with whom you know or even suspect you are somewhat incompatible, hoping that, sooner rather than later, you'll *become* compatible. We can't even count the times we have heard couples tell us, "I thought I could change him/her." You know what we've *never* heard? "I *did* change him/her!"

If something about your significant other bugs you now, it will bug you even more ten years from now. Malcolm and Laura didn't marry their clones, but they married their complements. Though they knew they would never be alike, they also believed they'd be stronger by joining their differences.

In *The Sacred Search* Gary wrote, "I know you love your boyfriend or girlfriend. But do you also *like* them? Are they the kind of person you enjoy being around? If it wasn't for the sexual chemistry, and if you didn't feel romantically inclined toward them, would you still enjoy their company?"

There are numerous tests that evaluate personality. At Second Baptist in Houston, Texas, we use "Prepare and Enrich," which I've (Gary) found very helpful. In addition to going through this study, I recommend that the two of you take this test or one like it. Remember, it's not about seeking sameness, but rather compatibility—someone you are *eager to live with*, not *willing to put up with*.

YOUR COVENANT MARRIAGE

We live in a time when the word *covenant* is all but absent from our daily vocabulary. It's interesting that the diminished use of this word mirrors the increase of divorce both inside and outside the church. A covenant is much more than a promise—it involves a binding and even sacred agreement between two individuals made before, and therefore calling upon, God.

The Bible mentions seven different covenants that God made with humankind. Interestingly, none of the covenants—not one—was dependent upon any of the people fulfilling their end of the agreement. Instead, God promised to fulfill His agreement no matter what anyone else in the covenant eventually did. A covenant relationship has its origins in this faith-based, principle-driven commitment between two parties with the Lord serving as the binding agent.

The idea of a covenant takes marriage to an entirely new level, regardless of our partner's actions. (Admittedly, the Bible does describe two instances when a person's actions are so egregious that

God declares the covenant can—but not must—be broken.) Divorce was very common in the society in which Jesus lived, but Jesus made it clear that *His* people would be marked by an entirely different style of life—when they got married, *they would stay married for life.* This is because (as Jesus stated in Matthew 19:3–6) marriage is about more than what two people decide to do or what a civil court declares has happened. In God's eyes, marriage is about what *He* does: God takes two people and somehow spiritually turns them into *one.* In one sense, this can never be undone, at least not without consequences. Jesus said in Matthew 5:31–32, "It has been said, 'Anyone who divorces his wife must give her a certificate of divorce.' But I tell you that anyone who divorces his wife, except for marital unfaithfulness, causes her to become an adulteress, and anyone who marries the divorced woman commits adultery."

Jesus said this when adultery was a capital offense. His words must have been shocking to the Jews, who held a much less exalted notion of marriage. Jesus all but obliterated any idea of His followers adopting the notion of "starter" marriages or seeking divorces merely because of disappointment or regret.

An individual who truly covenants with another doesn't break the commitments made or the vows exchanged. This person is determined to uphold his or her end of the bargain because that's what he or she agreed to do. The strength of a covenant marriage, therefore, rests on the promises made before God—not just the promises you made to each other. The primary motivation for your marital bond and commitment is God first, then your spouse, and always in that order.

God's design for marriage is why we're asking you to consider divorcing the concept of divorce when thinking about your future.

God didn't plan for divorce as any part of His original creation of marriage and family. Jesus didn't condone it, and any "exceptions" are to be weighed extremely carefully because of the serious consequences divorce will have on everyone. When you enter marriage with this perspective, your plan is to stay married and work to avoid any and all threats to your marriage, "so help you God." You and your spouse are committing to work through good times and bad, to be there for one another "in sickness and in health," and to protect the sacred bond that you will commit to in front of your family and friends on your wedding day.

Will things be perfect if you divorce the concept of divorce? Of course not—that's why you make a covenant before going in! You are both flawed sinners, so you can expect great days, okay days, and then some very, very bad days. There will be times of frustration and disappointment, but there will also be amazing seasons of closeness, romance, and sheer bliss. The strength of your union will be built and reinforced by how the two of you respond during the more difficult moments of marriage.

This also means there is tremendous security. When sin is exposed in either of your lives, as it will be, the two of you can work on the corresponding issues *together*, growing in Christ, learning to grant and seek forgiveness, within the security of a lifetime agreement. In this context, you figure out how to help each other grow in the very place where weakness is revealed instead of hiding from each other because you're afraid your partner might flee. You will learn to address issues as a single unit, because in God's eyes you are a team, sealed by a covenant. Marriage has been designed to be the ultimate interpersonal experience, a lifetime journey in learning how to work things out as a couple.

Before agreeing to enter into something as solemn and binding as a marriage covenant, you should check and recheck your commitment before you walk into it. God doesn't command you to *get* married, but once you choose to marry, He does intend for you to *stay* married. Marriage isn't like buying a car, where if it's not to your liking you can put a few miles on it and then trade it in one or two years later. (You don't make a covenant with a car!) You're going to live with this decision for the rest of your life. If things go bad, you're going to have to give all you've got to make things go right. Starting over shouldn't be a strategy you're even thinking about at this moment.

As enamored with each other as you are now, once you are married the day will come when one or both of you begin to have doubts and frustrations. This will happen; it's not a matter of if, it's a matter of when. So it's important that you enter into marriage with someone who agrees with you that biblical divorce is rarely an option and never a part of God's perfect plan. The questions in this session are designed to elicit further thoughts on the reality and permanence of marriage, to see just how committed you are to a divorce-is-not-an-option covenant marriage.

1. Are you prepared and willing to covenant to one another when it comes to marriage?

2. What would constitute a breach of such a covenant? List and share all exceptions and examples.

3. How permanent are marital vows, in your view?

4. Do you believe you're marrying someone who is committed to not just remain in, but also *work on* your marriage for the rest of your lives, even when he or she becomes disappointed in you or grows disenchanted with you? What makes you think your fiancé/fiancée is that kind of person?

5. Is there a history of divorce in your family? Describe and discuss each occurrence. What impact have these divorces had on you? What impact has divorce had on other family members? No superficial answers here. Be specific and detailed.

6. If your marriage hits a difficult time and your spouse feels frustrated and isn't finding satisfying resolution, will you commit to professional clinical counseling for as long as it takes to resolve the conflict? If not, why not?

7. When the two of you become frustrated with each other, what will be the most appropriate way for your spouse to address this frustration and receive constructive guidance? In other words, is it okay for your spouse to talk with his or her parents? A friend? Which one(s)? A pastor? What support system are you willing to develop for the success of your marital covenant?

8. Imagine yourself ten years from now. Your marriage has felt rather difficult for the last year. You've felt your spouse pulling away or just not being there anymore. Circumstances have changed. This is not what you signed up for. Finally, your spouse comes to you and says, "I know what we agreed to before we got married, but I've changed my mind. I want a divorce." How would you respond?

(Answer question 9 only after you and your fiancé/fiancée have discussed question 8 with your mentor.)

9. How does hearing how your fiancé/fiancée would respond make you feel now?

10. Having read about marriage being a covenant, does this covenant make you *more* or *less* excited about marriage? Why?

11. Given the permanence of marriage, do you think there are any aspects of your current relationship that need to be worked out before you make such a commitment?

12. As already stated, beyond making *personal* vows, beyond signing a *legal* document, biblical marriage is about making a covenant before God. Just as you will sign your name on a paper that will be registered with the state in which you will be married, will you sign your name in the presence of God to a vow that says you will not, under any circumstances, seek a divorce for anything other than a "biblical exception" (or the exceptions arising from those that the two of you

have discussed here in these conversations)? If so, please write that vow here, and then sign and date it. Please note that you are agreeing to this vow *on the day you get married*, not today. This does not grant you a biblical marriage! No head starts here, so please word your vow accordingly: "When I marry you, I am agreeing to …"

If this lesson leaves you sober minded, and it should, live with that heaviness for a while. Make sure you're willing to enter into such a holy and weighty agreement with this particular person. You haven't gotten married to each other yet, and if the thought of permanent marriage makes you second-guess your initial declaration, you can still responsibly leave the dating relationship and proceed as friends. Remember: Jesus taught the lifelong permanence of marriage.

DIVORCE DIVORCE

"I hate divorce," says the LORD *God of Israel.*
—Malachi 2:16

God's words "I hate divorce" aren't just indicative of His feelings; they're prophetic. We've talked to many people who have experienced divorce in some way, and they almost always end up saying the exact same words: "I just *hate* divorce and what it does."

Kids hate having to choose which parent to live with or watching one parent move out. Fathers and mothers hate not being able to spend every day with their children anymore. Many ex-spouses hate seeing their former partner walking hand in hand with someone else. Even if they feel the divorce was necessary or inevitable, they hate having to go through it.

Because of the way God made us, the way God made marriage, divorce is a horrific experience so toxic that no matter what the circumstances, it will leave radioactivity everywhere. God Himself hates it, and so should we.

But divorce reaches far beyond what it does to the two adult partners. If you hope to have children someday, you need to know going in how devastating divorce is to children. As counselors, we are tired of hearing comments like "the children will learn to cope," or "in the end it will all be for the best," or "given the circumstances, there was nothing else we could do." We need to recognize and embrace the great harm to children whenever a marriage fails, in part to help them heal.

Steve's doctoral dissertation focused on how adult children are frequently more devastated than younger children and take far longer to overcome the impact of divorce. In fact, Steve found that the older the kids were at the time of divorce, the more devastated and damaged they were by the divorce. Author Jen Abbas expressed this very experience in her book *Generation Ex:* "As I entered adulthood … I was stunned to discover that my parents' divorces seemed to affect me *more* each year, not less…. When they divorced, they may have thought they made a clean break, but we are the splintered remains of their parting. Regardless of *why* our parents divorced, the fact remains that their divorce hurt us."[1]

Jen made it so very clear: you may be able to give your kids a dozen different reasons why you're seeking a divorce, but in the end the divorce will *still* hurt enormously. Your reasons will never erase their pain. According to Jen, "Divorce is often *the* defining event of our life … the Achilles' heel to our well-being."[2]

1 Jen Abbas, *Generation Ex: Adult Children of Divorce and the Healing of Our Pain* (Colorado Springs: WaterBrook Press, 2004), 1–2.

2 Abbas, 12, 16.

Think of all that you want your future children to be "defined" by, all that you hope they will remember. How tragic that the one event they might use to describe their childhood, more than any other, would be a divorce.

We're sure you desire, as all parents do, that your future children's home will be a place of nurturing, healing, growth, and faith, a place where your kids can return every evening in order to rest, be encouraged, and built back up to face a painful, fallen world. When divorce takes place, however, the chaos is unleashed from within. Jen wrote, "Home is more likely to be the place where our most serious emotional wounds were inflicted."[3]

Since you are not married yet, this is your opportunity to make sure you're not entering a relationship that carries such destructive potential. Business experts say that the best time to fire someone is before you hire them. Don't get entangled with someone who eventually you hope to break away from (or who will easily break away from you).

You're not just choosing a spouse: you're choosing your kids' future mom or dad. And the stability of their childhood home will be based on the stability of your future spouse's character, faithfulness, and commitment to God. Does that encourage you or make you wary?

If you realize how devastating divorce is, you'll work that much harder to choose to marry someone for whom divorce is not an option. The sad reality is that one partner can bring a marriage to an end. We live in the world of no-fault divorce, and if you marry

---

3 Abbas, 88.

someone who is not as committed to marriage as you are, who doesn't share your values, who is willing to put their pleasure above their children's welfare, you may find yourself hugging teary-eyed children who are crying out in the middle of the night because they miss their mom or dad.

God hates divorce, and the easiest way to avoid a divorce is to make a wise marital choice. Let's divorce divorce from our own families by being thoughtful before we even get married.

AND THE TWO SHALL BECOME ONE

The woman speaking to me was frantic, trying unsuccessfully to hold it together while breaking out in fits of weeping and sighing, fearful that she was on the brink of lapsing into another nervous breakdown.

The cause of all this concern?

Her husband.

To whom she had been married for less than a year.

This isn't the place to get into the details of what was going on in their relationship, but one of the root causes was a lack of intimate oneness. In fact, her husband was upset that she couldn't come up with "her half of the rent" for that month.

"What do you mean *your* half of the rent?" I asked. "Aren't you married?"

"Yes," she replied, "but that's the way we do it."

On another occasion, Lisa and I sat across the table from a different couple, also married less than a year, facing one of their first unresolved marital crises. They were about to receive their first joint tax refund, and they wanted us to referee how much each spouse would receive. The very notion confused me. "Well," the wife explained, "my husband thinks that since he earned sixty percent of the income, he should get sixty percent of the refund. I think it should be fifty-fifty."

The way God designed marriage, there is no 60-40 or even 50-50. It's 100-100—"For this reason a man will leave his father and mother and be united to his wife, and they will become *one flesh*" (Gen. 2:24).

Biblical marriage is an "all in" proposition. Everything you have, you give to your spouse. Everything your spouse has, he or she gives to you. This includes all your possessions, your calendars (your time), your bodies, *everything*. Once you become one, there's no hiding at all. You can't biblically hoard "your" money or treat it as your own, regardless of whose name is on the front of the check. You can't act like you set your own schedule and then give your spouse the leftovers. You can't stop talking to your spouse just because you don't feel like it.

If two people are one, everything you do affects the other. This somewhat shocking oneness—two people, now considered one unit—is what getting married implies you're agreeing to. And that's what any biblically principled person or mentor will *hold* you to after the wedding.

No one can or should force you to give so much of yourself to someone else. No one can or should force you to become one with another person. But once you freely make that choice, you have no right to withhold or refuse to *become* one.

This might sound scary, but if you value intimacy, it should also sound delightful. Knowing and being known like this deeply satisfies our souls. It can be healing. It can be so fulfilling. It can be fun. It feels miraculous at times when two people, married a long time, say virtually the same thing at virtually the same time. It's comforting to know that our spouses have our backs and we have theirs. There's great security in knowing that no one will be allowed to come between us, that what we have is sacred and solid.

It's one thing to stand up on your wedding day and say, "I'll become one with you." It's another thing to wake up every day after that and follow through. Agreeing to marry is agreeing to become one *and to keep growing together as one.* My problems become *our* problems. My debts become *our* debts. Your illness becomes *our* illness. It's fraud to say, "I'll marry you" and then hold back from the responsibilities of marriage after the ceremony.

While the Bible says that marriage makes this oneness a declared reality, in human experience it's also a gradual *process* that we either cultivate or resist. The problem arises because, in our flesh, many of us want the benefits of intimacy without paying the price to get there. We want everything our spouse has, but we want to hold back a little of what we have for ourselves. (You can have my time, but not my Friday nights. You can influence some of our financial decisions, but that inheritance is *mine*. You can have sex with me when I'm in the mood for it, but not unless I can't think of anything better to do.)

Marriage doesn't work this way; we're either one or we're not. Half of a marriage is not enough of a marriage for most people. And most marital problems arise because people are trying to maintain a part-time commitment and eventually finding that it's not worth the bother.

By agreeing to marry each other, you are establishing a priority of commitment: your calendar is no longer your own. Your money is no longer your own. Whether or how you take care of your body is no longer solely up to you. Somebody else has a vested interest in you and all aspects of your life.

This is exciting. By answering and discussing these very questions, the two of you can begin the lifelong journey of becoming one.

1. In a relationship based on oneness, do you believe there are any acceptable secrets? If so, please list them and discuss each one with your mentor.

2. How do you feel about sharing email, Facebook, and any other passwords? Why?

3. How do you feel about having all financial matters in common? Explain.

4. One of the primary tools for becoming one is communication. Will you agree to spend a significant amount of time in relational conversation with your spouse? And how do you define significant? How often? What should the interval be?

5. Will you agree ahead of time to reject any form of the silent treatment or stonewalling to resolve conflict? If not, why not?

6. Describe what makes you feel most connected to your fiancé/fiancée.

(Answer question 7 only after you and your fiancé/fiancée have discussed questions 1 through 6 with your mentor.)

7. Having heard your fiancé/fiancée's answers, are such actions something you are willing to practice *for the rest of your life*?

8. Is there an area in your relationship that you can currently identify as the strongest threat against building a sense of oneness, or perhaps an issue that will make becoming one problematic? If so, what is it?

9. Are you willing to "leave" your family (make your future spouse a higher priority) *and* make your fiancé/fiancée's extended family just as high a priority as your own? What will be most difficult about this?

10. How will your friendships with other people change after you get married? Think about his relationships … Now, think about hers …

11. Will both of you agree to attend the same church? Which one? Which kind?

12. Having considered the issue of marital oneness, is there anything your fiancé/fiancée needs to know about your present or your past

that they don't know but should (financial entanglements, sexual history, physical disabilities/issues, family conflicts, past relationships, ongoing struggles with sin, mental illness)? If so, will you commit to discuss any and all of these specifics with your marriage mentor now or at your next session?

MOVING TOWARD EACH OTHER

Many years ago, Lisa and I (Gary) went to see a movie with two of our closest friends, Rob and Jill. At the start of the movie, I sat by Rob and Lisa sat by Jill, so that Lisa and Jill could share the unbuttered popcorn and Rob and I could assault our arteries with the buttered kind. But halfway through the movie, Lisa had to get up for a moment, and Rob slipped over to sit by his wife.

There was something wonderfully refreshing in seeing a man who had been married for almost two decades still eager to sit by his wife for the last hour of a movie. That simple movement said a great deal about Rob and Jill's marriage, and it exemplifies a biblical truth.

Marriage is more than a static commitment; it is a *dynamic movement* toward someone. Men, will you commit, as future husbands, to keep moving toward your wives? The most frequent complaint we hear from brides of all ages is that while their fiancés seemed so "into them" before the wedding, once the wedding was over they suddenly developed a new interest in lowering their golf handicap, getting a promotion at work, or reengaging in a time-consuming hobby. There's just something about the male psyche that thinks, "I've got the girl—what's the next challenge?"

We have to be aware of this and resist it. Never settle in, assuming you know your love as well as she can be known. She's going to change: getting married will change her. Having children (or facing infertility) will change her. Getting older will change her. You've got to keep pursuing your spouse or risk becoming a stranger to the person you married. And few things are as sad as that. Are you ready to make this kind of commitment to this particular woman?

Women, will you commit to keep moving toward your husband? Even after you have children? Many young moms fall into the trap of becoming moms first and wives second. They've "got their man" and presume on his commitment, faithfulness, and affection. A lot of relational damage can be done if you put your marriage and your oneness at risk.

Are you willing to share your spouse's successes and failures, even if he or she bores you or (in the case of failures) tempts you to think less of him or her? Will you become your mate's critic, or will you recognize an opportunity to bolster his or her confidence and build your spouse back up? Will you consider new ways to please and pleasure each other? Are you prepared to do this *for the rest of your life*?

Jesus moved toward us even in our sin: "While we were still sinners, Christ died for us" (Rom. 5:8). Will you commit to move toward your future spouse even in his or her sin? Will you learn to forgive, fight through the hurt and pain, and resolve that the two of you will face any challenge or character flaw, whatever it is, *together*, and keep building your marriage?

Will you agree to pursue intimacy even when it's uncomfortable? Will you courageously seek to resolve conflict, or will you grow weary or lazy and push the relationship aside, assuming it's "not worth the hassle" while letting your love grow cold? Will you make the time to listen, and will you make the effort to understand your spouse's world, his or her temptations and trials, frustrations and challenges, without getting so wrapped up in your own life and challenges that you ignore your spouse's?

Your marriage may not begin for some time, but your relationship can point toward oneness and intimacy right now. Make a commitment that you want to end every month knowing your partner a little bit better than you knew him or her the month before. Why not make a renewed attempt to study your spouse every bit as much as an astronomy student studies the stars? Why not, as some couples have done, begin writing a "book of _____ " (your future spouse's name) where you write down things you learn about your spouse, what they like, what they don't like, helping you to give serious thought and reflection to becoming a better lover, friend, brother or sister in Christ?

Becoming one isn't like falling in love. Infatuation happens just by showing up; intimate oneness takes effort, intention, and perseverance.

BUILDING A FAMILY

A famous CEO thought he was being hired to run a car company. He thought his work would be focused on producing exciting new automobiles, but after a year of running the company he confessed that sometimes he felt like he spent most of his time running a health and pension plan for the employees.

It's common that we enter into a new enterprise expecting one thing, only to find out that it's mostly about something else.

The same is true of love and romance. Couples get married because they want to be together, they want to be a *couple*, but most couples don't stay couples. They become *families* with one or more children.

While there have been a few couples we've met over the years who had predetermined that they weren't going to have children, most people entering marriage plan on making a family together at some point in the future (and even those that don't sometimes end up with one). Yet the percentage of couples who actually discuss the *details* of putting a family together, pre-engagement or pre-marriage, is typically small. We believe this is another essential aspect of conversation that must take place as you get ready to launch yourself into marriage.

Creating a family begins with your vision of what you hope your family will look like one day. Do you want to have one, two, three, or more children? What if infertility becomes a problem? We've seen an increased number of couples enter counseling because of this painful situation and the marital issues it brings up, yet few premarital couples have ever had in-depth conversations before their wedding day about what they would do if faced with infertility.

These conversations lead to other critical questions: do you want to adopt kids or take in foster children? Do your two visions of the future and your family match up? What if one or both of you already has a child? What will your blended family look like—who will have custody, and are you comfortable with all your kids living together?

In addition to these fundamental conversations, the concept of how you will parent must be part of the dialogue. Do you believe in a strict style of parenting, or will you be easygoing with your kids? How were you raised by your own parents? Did you like and/or agree with their style of parenting? How would you change things? What does your partner think about these same questions and concerns?

There is also the reality that your children may have their own sets of challenges. For instance, many families must adjust to a child who has a physical, emotional, mental, or psychological problem. These kinds of issues will affect not only your parenting but also your marital relationship.

While parenting may seem a long way off, kids can enter the picture at any time. Unfortunately, we've seen far too many couples come in for counseling who were underprepared for the role of parenting. Many complaints arise about the other spouse's approach to discipline or their lack of involvement in the parenting process. Yet when asked if they had ever talked about these matters before marriage, the most common answer (by far) is a simple no.

Now is the time to engage in high-quality conversations about what you'd like your family to look like and how you will both manage the stress that comes with parenting. The questions in this session are designed to get you past thinking about merely becoming a couple, and start thinking about establishing a family.

1. If you were going to hire someone to raise your kids with you—and their only job was to be your kids' dad or mom—what traits would you want them to have?

2. Which of these traits do you have? Which do you believe your fiancé/fiancée excels in?

3. Are there any traits you believe your fiancé/fiancée will need to develop more fully in order to serve as an effective parent? If so, what are they?

4. How badly do you want to have children?

> _ I wouldn't marry someone if they wouldn't agree to have children.
> _ My preference would be to have kids, but that's negotiable.
> _ I do not want to have kids, but I'm willing to consider them if my spouse wants them.
> _ I will not, under any circumstances, choose to become a parent.

5. How many children do you want to have?

6. When would you like to begin having children? Do you care how far they are spaced apart?

7. What will be the positives of having your fiancé/fiancée's parents as your children's grandparents?

8. What will be the primary challenges of having your fiancé/fiancée's parents serve as your children's grandparents?

9. About one in six couples struggle with infertility. If the two of you prove to be one of those couples, what medical technologies would you be willing to use to assist you in having children, and which would you definitely *not* choose? If you're not familiar with this list, you may need to do some research to answer the question:

- Surrogacy
- In vitro fertilization
- Egg donation
- Sperm donation
- The use of fertility drugs to treat ovulation disorders

10. Some of the above treatments can be quite expensive. Which of the following best describes your attitude toward this expense?

_ I would spend whatever it takes to conceive, even if it means going into debt.
_ I would spend as much as we are able, but not if it means going into debt.

_ I would want to wait a very long time before spending serious money to get help conceiving a child.

_ If we can't conceive "naturally," I would not be willing to spend any money trying to treat our infertility.

11. If you aren't able to have any biological children, would you like to adopt? Does it matter what country you adopt from?

12. Even if you can produce biological offspring, is adoption something you'd like to pursue?

13. Do you believe day care is an acceptable option for raising your children? If the answer is no, who do you expect will stay home with the children, or will that be shared? How?

14. Do you have a philosophy of child rearing, such as spanking or not spanking, raising them up in a particular faith, public/private/home schooling, other issues?

15. Describe the ideal home/neighborhood in which you'd like to raise your kids. Is it in a city or the suburbs or the country? Is it a large house with a large yard, or perhaps a smaller home with no yard? Don't let finances dictate your answer here; write down what you think the ideal environment would be.

16. Is there any city or environment in which you absolutely would not live? If so, what/where?

17. Who will be your children's guardians if something happens to you?

18. If you give your future spouse a 10 on a scale of 1 to 10 for how well they suit you to be a husband or wife, how would you grade them on how well you think they'll do to become a father/mother?

(Answer question 19 only after you and your fiancé/fiancée have discussed the previous questions with your mentor.)

19. Given your fiancé/fiancée's answers in this chapter, does he or she seem like a wise choice for someone with whom you will raise a family? Why or why not?

SOMEDAY

A character in a movie once said, "For most men, a woman's body is the most beautiful thing they will ever see." A female character asked, "What's the most beautiful thing a girl sees?" The first character responded, "Her first child."[1]

We want to take you on an imagination tour. Go forward with us five or ten or fifteen years from now. "Children" are no longer theoretical to you; they're real flesh-and-blood residents in your home. They make noise, they create messes, they consume large amounts of money and soil large numbers of diapers and clothes. But you love them. Oh, how you love them. You would die for them without even having to contemplate the cost. You would do anything you could to make their lives better.

On that day, you will want them to have the absolutely best parents they could ever have. You will either be so thankful that you've given them your spouse as a dad or mom, or you will be regretful over who is sharing the task with you.

1   *Venus*, directed by Roger Michell (New York: Miramax Films, 2006).

Right now, you're not only *choosing* your future children's parent, but you're shaping your children's future parent. The way you encourage your fiancé/fiancée, the way you help them grow in their faith, or the way you ignore serious issues "just to get along" is either helping your future kids' parent grow, or it's setting the stage for a disappointing performance.

Why not spend a few days talking about how the two of you can encourage each other to grow for the sake of your future children? Talk about the kind of mom or dad you want to be; discuss what you don't want to be like and what you might have to do to avoid acting that way. Do you think you might need some counseling? Are there some relational skills you need to learn? Do you think you need to get more serious about addressing bad habits? Do you need to look at health issues?

You're not just becoming a couple; in most instances, you're starting a *family*. You can prepare for that now. For instance, how can you build a common faith so that your shared devotion to Christ will be a shelter for your children and a natural invitation for them to follow Christ as well? Are you in a solid church? Are you growing in your love for the Word of God? Are you finding opportunities to serve? Are there any problems in your faith (lack of prayer, discipline, etc.)?

Are you making financial plans to support a family? Are you spending everything you have on expensive vacations or cars, or are you being careful to increase your savings in case a child comes along a little earlier than expected?

Are you making wise health choices, realizing that being a parent is tough physically and requires you to be in the best shape possible? You'll want to be active, not just for children but for your grandchildren, and the health choices you make now could have a huge influence on that. It's much easier to address eating and exercise issues before you become a parent—your schedule will be put through a blender once you're caring for an infant, giving you far less freedom about what you can prepare to eat or when you can exercise.

Discuss these issues in an encouraging way, not to act like your future spouse needs to step it up, but rather to ask, "How can we help each other grow to one day become the best parents we could be?" In trying to become the best parents, you're learning how to help each other become better people. If you can do this in an encouraging way, you're going to experience one of the purposes of marriage—two people becoming more like Christ.

CONSTRUCTIVE CONFLICT

Bobby and Jacalyn took the personality test our church provides to all engaged couples and proved to be almost completely compatible. Seriously, I (Gary) have never had a couple who seemed more made for each other than these two. Bobby confessed, "The only thing we really fight about is who loves each other the most."

But even Bobby and Jacalyn are going to have issues come up that will have to be resolved. Conflict is certain. The fact that there will be conflict in your marriage doesn't mean there's something wrong with your marriage—it just means your spouse is still alive. Conflict is a reality in all aspects of life because it involves differing opinions, values, beliefs, and behavior patterns. If you simply put two people in a room, eventually they will be in conflict about something. So why would you expect complete harmony in your marriage? Why would you be disappointed and discouraged when conflict occurs?

If you want to succeed and *enjoy* your marriage, you're going to have to learn not to be afraid of conflict and even appreciate its necessary role in building a relationship. Since a conflict-free marriage is not possible, the *resolution* of conflict should be our focus, and that begins with a basic understanding of how most people typically attempt to resolve differences and disagreements in their lives.

The majority of men and women will fall into one of two camps: *fight* or *flight*. There are some people who can't wait for an argument or dispute, but there are others who run from any sign of a clash or quarrel. The probability that you and your partner will each fall into one of these camps is high.

In business, conflict creates losses in time, productivity, and profitability. In marriage, unresolved conflict can eventually lead to disrespect, division, and even divorce. Learning to embrace the reality of conflict in our lives is the first step toward being more successful and satisfied in all of our relationships. Couples must learn to identify their tendency toward fight or flight and then find a healthy way to address situations kindly and gently rather than falling back on anger or avoidance.

One of the optimal methods for finding resolution is establishing a set of principles about how conflict will be resolved in your relationship. Sitting down and actually writing these principles out is a good starting place, and then you can discuss those guidelines together to ensure they will work for both of you. Once you've set up these guidelines to resolve conflict, start following them every time you have a disagreement. It only takes one hole to sink a ship; in the same way, one unresolved conflict can let in enough bitterness to sink an entire marriage. Avoidance, repression, and denial cannot be part of this process if you hope to grow through conflict rather than be crushed by it.

Sometimes couples need the help of mentors, pastors, and professional counselors to learn how to understand their past style of dealing with conflict and make the changes necessary for healthy, productive, and satisfying interactions and relationships. Don't be afraid to seek and get the assistance you need—sooner rather than later. The longer you live and the more successful you are, the more conflict you will have. Our goal is never to have a conflict-free zone. Instead, we strive to develop a common set of values and principles by which we can establish a conflict-resolution zone that works best for us.

Finally, forgiveness must be part of resolving conflict. When you truly have reached a place of forgiveness, three key elements should be included in the process:

- You commit to letting go of the conflict or problem. When it comes to mind, you refocus on other things and refuse to dwell upon the hurt.
- You don't talk to the offending person about it ever again.
- You never talk to anyone else about it ever again outside of a professional context (professional counselor, pastor, physician, etc.).

This is a high standard for forgiveness. Many men and women bail out and will not commit to such a standard because they are committed to hanging on to their anger. We ask large groups of people regularly to give us a single good reason to refuse to grant forgiveness. To date, after thirty-plus years of such surveys, we have yet to hear a single acceptable answer. There simply are no good reasons not to apply the three elements of forgiveness listed above. Remember, marriage is a team sport. While conflict will be a reality, your ultimate goal should be the unity of your couple/family unit. In other words, you can lose an awful lot by "winning" a marital argument. It's not about winning; it's about loving, understanding, forgiving, and growing in intimacy.

1. Describe how your parents usually handled conflict. Was there a lot of yelling? Were issues ignored or buried? How about the silent treatment, abusive language, or even violence? Try to write out an accurate description of what you grew up with.

2. How did your parents' experiences with conflict affect you and how you resolve conflict today?

3. On a scale of one to ten, rank where you land between "fight" and "flight" during relational conflict, particularly in regards to your current relationship:

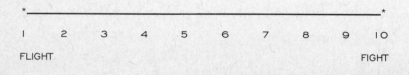

| 1 | 2 | 3 | 4 | 5 | 6 | 7 | 8 | 9 | 10 |
| FLIGHT | | | | | | | | | FIGHT |

4. Let's dig a little deeper, beyond a number. Does conflict scare you, frustrate you, or excite you? When you think about conflict, what comes to mind regarding your personal reaction? Why do you think this is so?

5. What do you think a *healthy* approach to conflict would look like? In an ideal marriage, how would you and your spouse deal with disagreements?

Read James 4:1–3:

> Those conflicts and disputes among you, where do they come from? Do they not come from your cravings that are at war within you? You want something and do not have it; so you commit murder. And you covet something and cannot obtain it; so you engage in disputes and conflicts. You do not have, because you do not ask. You ask and do not receive, because you ask wrongly, in order to spend what you get on your pleasures.
> (NRSV)

We encourage you to memorize this biblical passage and remind yourself of it whenever conflict arises.

6. How can you train yourself to look at what's going on in your own heart—the cravings that war within you, the frustration that you're not getting what you want, the possibility that you might be pursuing something with selfish or false motives—before you start attacking or challenging your spouse?

7. Based on James 4:1–3, do you believe it's possible to desire something that is essentially *good* (sexual intimacy, intimate communication, considerate respect, etc.) in a way that becomes sinful? If so, how so?

8. Describe the healthiest conflict resolution the two of you have experienced—a time when you disagreed yet grew from the experience.

9. Next, describe the most destructive conflict the two of you have experienced.

10. What was the difference? How can you have more of what you described in question 8 and less of what you described in question 9?

11. Will you commit, in the future, to pray about your own heart and desires first, before you ever ask God to change your spouse? Will you commit to ask God to show you the 10 percent where you're in error, even when you're convinced your spouse is 90 percent in the wrong? If you will do this, you will be amazed at how productive conflict can be, rather than so destructive and debilitating.

12. List five to ten principles that you will commit to follow every time you are involved in conflict. Share and discuss these with your marriage mentor.

When it comes to marital conflict, there are many unhealthy forms of communication—acts that make the conflict worse. Let's agree to reject all these unhealthy methods of relating:

a. *Hurtful words.* So much harm can be done in so little time if we don't train our tongues (see James 3:1–12). Name-calling or blasting back with hateful things has never solved a single marital conflict. It has never served the cause of love. It has never fostered intimacy.

b. *Stonewalling.* This is such a harmful and common practice. It's passive-aggressiveness taken to a malicious level. When you agree to marry someone, you agree ahead of time to work through conflict. Stonewalling (the silent treatment or withdrawal) is essentially renouncing your wedding vows. Some introverted personality types may need a moment to themselves to collect their thoughts and pray, but this is different from refusing to engage with your spouse. It's putting off resolution indefinitely, and that's just wrong.

c. *Bringing up the past.* Adopt this mantra: "One conflict at a time." There is no use trying to bring three previous fights into the current one.

d. *Acting like you're above being wrong.* In most conflicts, two people are both behaving inappropriately. One might be 95 percent in the wrong, but there is still 5 percent to be owned.

> Your spouse's 95 percent doesn't excuse your
> 5 percent. Seek to grow, not to win, in every
> argument. Own that 5 percent.

Your goal, as a couple, is to increase your understanding of each other, expand your own worldview (maybe your spouse sees something in you that you have been blind to), grow toward each other, seek the truth that is above us all, and do all this in a way that builds you up as individuals and as a couple. Conflict can be enormously beneficial when that's the result. This goes way beyond marriage. Learning to handle conflict in a godly way can increase your humility, understanding, gentleness, patience, and ability to forgive (an essential skill in a fallen world) in all relationships.

VACATION VANITY

Once the plane's wheels hit the ground, I (Gary) breathed a huge sigh of relief. It had been over eighteen months since I had taken a vacation. I was especially exhausted from a heavy travel schedule and an eight-hour flight, and I was looking forward to some quiet beach time and rest. A few books, a lounge chair, a cold drink nearby, and I'd be a very happy man indeed.

My wife walked off the same plane with a different agenda. We were in a new place—and we only had fourteen days to explore every corner and drive down every road. On our second full day, to get us off to a good start, she suggested a "few little stops." *Twelve hours later*, we arrived back at our condo, and my wife started talking about other things we could do in the remaining thirteen days.

"I can't afford to leave this place more exhausted than when I got here," I protested.

"It sounds like a lot to you," my wife answered, "but think of all the things I'm already leaving out!"

I had flown over a hundred thousand miles in the past twelve months and had been to over a dozen different states and three different countries. I wanted to regather my strength rather than expand my experience. My wife doesn't travel nearly as much as I do. The chance to be away is a chance for her to see and experience new things.

So who was right?

Both of us, of course. I had a legitimate need for relaxation, and my wife had a legitimate desire for exploration.

So who was wrong?

Both of us, of course. My wife should have known I needed more rest; I shouldn't have acted like my need for rest was more important than the family's need to do fun things together.

So how do you resolve something that can be looked at from either angle?

The answer is simple: humility.

Marriage books often dispense ready-made advice for how to resolve conflict, but there is usually a deeper issue at stake: sinful pride.

James was very clear when he wrote, "What causes fights and quarrels among you? Don't they come from your desires that battle within you? You want something but don't get it" (James 4:1–2).

My wife and I both had needs, and it just so happened (as it often does) that our needs were in conflict. We couldn't resolve them. We could try to split the difference down the middle—do something half of the days, rest the other half—but in all honesty, that was still sounding really busy to me and really boring to my wife.

The real problem was that both of us were using our own needs as the basis for what we thought the family should do. Pride can't be mollified; it must be crucified. As long as I acted like my needs were more important, and as long as my wife acted as if her desires were more important, we'd never reach a place of peace.

This was more than a little frustrating to me. I didn't fly halfway around the globe and spend several thousand dollars so that I could quarrel with my wife. We could do that at home for free!

Nevertheless, we spent the first three days in a Hawaiian paradise quarreling, compromising, and uneasily hammering out a loose agreement that the two of us were willing to live with. Neither one of us was really happy with the result. I didn't get near the amount of rest and recovery I was hoping for, and she didn't get to see half the places she wanted to see, but you know what?

Maybe the purpose of this vacation wasn't about me getting a certain amount of rest and my wife getting a certain amount of excitement.

Maybe God's agenda was to confront the pride that rules our hearts. God may not have been as concerned with what my wife and I deemed most important; He may well have been far more interested in both of us being shaped into the image of Christ: "Do nothing out of selfish ambition or vain conceit, but in humility consider others better than yourselves. Each of you should look not only to your own interests, but also to the interests of others. Your attitude should be the same as that of Christ Jesus" (Phil. 2:3–5).

It's precisely because I so desperately wanted rest that I needed to be challenged not to make my wants the determining factor of how my family would spend its time. And it's precisely because Lisa was so eager to do so much that the vacation afforded her such a powerful example of crucifying her own wants and learning to put someone else first.

Isn't it possible that God was more concerned about me growing in unselfishness than about me getting some rest? And isn't it also possible that God was more concerned that Lisa learn to think of the needs of someone else, even though she was so excited about seeing some new things?

If you don't enter marriage being willing to entertain these questions—if you don't see your pride as your greatest spiritual enemy, and Christlikeness as a worthy goal of your journey together—you'll get lost in the give-and-take of personal desires. That will spawn nothing but resentment, frustration, and alienation.

When two people desire to grow spiritually, conflict acts like an X-ray. It shows the "doctor" where the problem lies, what needs to be cut, or what medicine needs to be applied. When two people just want to be happy or to have someone else see things their way, conflict becomes a battle to be won or another fight to be avoided. That kills personal growth, and it eventually erodes intimacy in the marriage.

It's not until we crucify our pride and take on the same attitude as that of Christ Jesus that we can be freed to vacation with the ultimate purpose: allowing God to use a seemingly no-win situation in order to help two people both become more mature. In this sense, with neither of us getting exactly what we wanted, both of us won. God used a common event in life to accomplish His eternal purposes.

DEVELOPING AND MAINTAINING SEXUAL INTIMACY

The more we understand how sex works in the souls of a man and a woman, the more we marvel at God's brilliant design. *The Sacred Search* talks about this in more depth, but in general, sexual expression renews a husband's affections for his wife in a way that nothing else really does. It also provides numerous benefits to a wife's sense of well-being. For both men and women, a fulfilling sexual relationship within the covenant of marriage is a very healthy place to live.

Unfortunately, over time many couples grow bored with sexual expression. In the beginning of the sexual relationship, when the chemistry and desire are high and the thrill of something new is so strong, you may not have to work at it. Desire (absent some emotional, spiritual, or physical complications) won't be a problem.

But to enjoy *long-term* sexual satisfaction, you're going to have to be willing to work. Dr. Juli Slattery likens the gift of sex to a Legos set instead of a Tonka truck. The truck is ready made, a toy right out of the box. The Legos set becomes fun only as you build something with it—part of the enjoyment is putting it together. But then, after you've built it, it becomes boring unless you tear it apart and build something new.

Sexual intimacy in marriage is like that. You'll have one experience as newlyweds, but the relationship will change somewhat after your sexual relationship develops over the years. It will change even more when you start having babies, toddlers, teenagers, and then become middle-aged or older with some physical challenges. If you don't work at rebuilding sexual intimacy in these stages, it will be all too easy to drift apart sexually.

Why say all this now, even before you're married? To put you in the mind-set that sexual intimacy, as delightful and intense and wonderful as it is initially, requires some effort to build and maintain. If you think long-term sexual excitement and satisfaction is supposed to "just happen" and be easy and natural to maintain, you'll give up when you face inevitable difficulties. Sexual fulfillment is worth working for, but it *will* take some work. Sex is like a dance. Every couple must learn to dance together over time. The more they practice, communicate, and dance, the better the result.

The purpose of this session is to provide you with the tools needed to develop a great sex life and maintain this intimacy through the natural ups and downs of your life together. The beauty of sexual intimacy is that it will become an even richer part of your relationship when you and your spouse make it a priority in your marital journey.

There are three key points about sexual intimacy that we'd like you to begin thinking about:

1. A husband's and wife's individual sexuality directly affects their sexual satisfaction as a couple.

2. How you were raised in terms of your sexual development (neglectful/abusive/healthy) will impact marital sex and satisfaction.

3. Matters related to sexual identity, gender identity, hetero versus homosexuality, abortion(s), sexually transmitted diseases, etc., are among a list of historical experiences that will also affect marital sex and satisfaction.

As you will see in the questions that follow, we encourage you to be open and honest with each other as you discuss your sexual past. After three decades of counseling couples, we have found that most sexual problems and dissatisfaction have their foundation in sexual, emotional, and physical matters that go unresolved in one or both individuals in a marital relationship. Simply ignoring past experiences and problems or pretending they never happened doesn't make them go away—instead, these problems tend to fester and slowly erode sexual intimacy and the closeness you should be able to enjoy as a couple. The great news is that once many of these problems are addressed, many husbands and wives are able to fully enjoy their sexual experiences together with little or no impact from the past.

We know what you may be thinking: "If I open up about my past, especially sexual feelings and/or experiences, this person may not want to marry me!" Let's consider that thought, because you may be right. Once your potential spouse finds out what you think about sex, what your sexual past may or may not have been, and what your expectations for sexual intimacy are in the future, he or she may indeed decide not to marry you. By the way, the same may be equally true for you. You may decide that you can't handle what has happened in your loved one's life either.

But isn't this what you want to find out now—well before you get married, settle down, and start a family together? After all, if either of you simply can't get past something now, what makes you think that by keeping it a secret, it will be any better when one of you finds out about it later? (Which, by the way, usually happens whether we like it or not.)

And even more importantly, do you really want to be married to someone who can't accept you for who you really are? Remember the Pre-engagement Punch List in session 1? One of the foundational principles we shared is that each of you is a flawed sinner. You must accept this about each other now if you have any hope to live out a full, satisfying life together. So if you have had an abortion, your future mate should know about it. That's part of your past experience, your present feelings, who you are today, and how you'll look at life's tomorrows. Forgiven, yes. Fact of life? Definitely. If you've had a previous sexual partner(s), your present partner should know about it. Why? Because this too defines who you've become as a man or woman. Again, forgiven by God? Of course! But the reality of living in a fallen world means your spouse deserves to know who they are marrying.

Taking time to talk about these most intimate details of your lives now may seem and could actually be painful for a season, but the potential for developing an even deeper relationship with the person you plan to marry is exponential. Why? Because you are willing to let them see exactly who you are as a sexual being created in God's image—not perfect, but willing to perfect your sexual life with this person throughout your marital journey together. It's a scary door to open and enter, but the intimacy it can lead to is a wonderful place to live.

1. Write down the details about how the topic of sex was handled in the family you grew up in. In particular, be sure to address:

What were your parents'/caregivers' attitudes and beliefs about sex?

How were you educated about your own sexual development?

What moral values were you taught about your own sexual behavior?

2. It is time to discuss your sexual histories with each other in detail and with complete candor and honesty. Please remember, however,

that while it is important to share details, they should be "qualified details." For example, you and your potential spouse should learn about previous sexual partners, homosexual tendencies, abortions, sexually transmitted diseases, previous sexual abuse, and the like. Explicit details, however, such as "What was the sex like? How many times? What positions?" can be potentially harmful. Your marriage mentor will help you explore what you need to know without slipping into all you may want to know. Remember, this is not disclosure for the sake of therapy, where, in privacy, further detail might be professionally helpful. This is pre-marriage mentoring, helping you determine the wisdom of your choice and preparing the two of you to build the foundation for a strong marriage.

3. Which of the details or circumstances shared from your sexual history will make it most difficult for you to develop and maintain a healthy sexual relationship with your future spouse?

4. (This question will be answered only after you hear your partner's answers to questions 2 and 3.) Are you willing to accept these aspects of your partner's sexual history and also commit to never bring them up in a moment of anger or use these details to hurt them?

5. Discuss your expectations about your sexual needs. What do you prefer? What is out of the question? How will you address your spouse's desires and needs when they are uncomfortable for you? Do you ever expect there to be a time when sex won't be a part of your relationship?

6. How do you feel about reading appropriate literature or even talking to a counselor to improve this area of your marriage? As a couple, what strategies do you have for developing a sexually satisfying marriage?

7. If your partner finds himself/herself unsatisfied with your sexual relationship, what is the best way for him/her to communicate this to you in a constructive manner? While it's happening? Immediately after? The next day? What would be the best way to express it?

Addressing sexual dissatisfaction is a difficult thing to do, but doing so can benefit your marriage tremendously. Working through sexual issues will require you to grow in the virtues of courage, humility, empathy, understanding, and clear communication. All of these qualities will serve to improve the quality of your marriage relationally, spiritually, and emotionally. Ignoring sexual issues will increase fear, arrogance, tempt you to hide or build a "double life," foster self-centeredness, and incline you toward avoiding other tough issues. We might wish sex was always perfect, and that two people would just "know" how to please each other, but the relational work required to build long-term sexual satisfaction is actually great practice for building intimacy in all areas of marriage.

8. Are you concerned in any way about your ability to please your future spouse sexually? If yes, please describe what those concerns might be.

9. Because of your past or personal issues, are there any aspects of normal marital sexuality that you simply do not believe you could participate in or feel it would be unwise for you to engage in?

10. What do you want your future spouse to know about that would make your wedding night/honeymoon most special for you? What

expectations do you have for yourself? What fears do you have, if any?

11. When it comes to your sexual satisfaction in marriage, what are the three things you most want your future spouse to know about you and your desires?

THE POWER OF A PURE PASSION

As an engineer, God hit this one out of the park.

Creating a physical act that literally, through the chemical reactions in our brains, renews marital affection, costs nothing, offers tremendous physical pleasure in a world filled with frequent pain, becomes a shared and exclusive experience that protects the stability of the entire family—just from a creative perspective, how can we not be in awe of the amazing invention of God that our culture describes by that little three-letter word *sex*?

When Christians begin to understand the role, importance, and blessing of healthy marital sexuality, that it has the potential to become such a positive, holy force for good, they will embrace it with a new enthusiasm and sense of purpose. Experiencing sexual intimacy on this level will help us to fully live out God's design for intimacy, creating such a powerful experience that any thought of infidelity is shut out. In fact, positive sexual experience is like pulling the weeds of temptation from the ground; they're removed before they have a chance to grow.

How can couples use the power of sex to keep them together through all seasons of marriage? Here are just two quick thoughts.

1. KEEP IT EXCLUSIVE

If you're ever frustrated with your sexual relationship, the worst thing you can do is to "cope" with a substitute—trashy novels and television programs, pornography, or an affair. Every marriage is going to endure some dry spells. You can respond by learning to communicate with each other on deeper levels, becoming vulnerable and open to change, growing in empathy, and being committed to meeting each other's needs. Or you can take the "easy" way out by falling into the trap of settling for a readily available substitute, in which case sex will surely pull you apart. Remember the bonding power of sex—something really positive when it connects two spouses, but extremely destructive when it causes one spouse to bond with something or someone outside the home.

Shortcuts often become habits. What gets you through the night can be used to weather a difficult month and then endure a challenging year. Pretty soon, you'll realize you've developed an addiction and feel alienated from and bitter toward your spouse.

For sex to work the way God intended it to, we must preserve the exclusive nature of marital sexuality—in thought, word, and deed (and that begins now, even before you're married). When sex begins to wane, your sexual drive and frustration is God's physical reminder that you need to pay *more* attention to your marriage, not less. Use your energy to address the frustrating issues in your marriage instead of ignoring your problems and making them worse yet by "coping" with a substitute.

2. MAKE AN EFFORT

Since sex is a good gift, blessed by God, with so many positive benefits, it is our privilege to put time, thought, and effort into making it happen—in terms of quality as well as quantity.

With small kids, tight budgets, and privacy issues, a lack of intentionality is going to erode any sexual relationship. To be honest, most seasons of marriage won't afford you the opportunity to create a "grand slam" sexual experience as often as you would like. Intentionality, creativity, and understanding your current circumstances will bring perspective and appreciation instead of accusation and resentment. Mutual sexual unity is the product of a covenant team of two maintaining their intimacy throughout life's journey.

You may wish you had a better body to give your spouse; you may lament your lack of sexual skill or the amount of energy you possess at the end of the day. But more important than these concerns—and even more of a blessing—is to earnestly become a *generous* lover, bringing the kindness of Christ to your spouse in a very physical and, yes, pleasurable way.

We know some wonderful Christian counselors who specialize in sexual issues. It is their contention that it takes a couple about twenty years to truly master the art of mutual sexual fulfillment. Initial sexual chemistry is intense, but it won't last. Learning how to truly please, serve, and receive can take time.

In the midst of all this, never forget that satisfying sex isn't just about you and your spouse. It's not just about affair-proofing your marriage. It's about pleasing the ultimate engineer, the God who thought it all up in the first place. And for a believer, there is no greater joy than that.

MONEY, MONEY, MONEY

When you marry someone, you not only marry their money, you also marry their debt, their credit score and history, their view of charity, their philosophy of savings and investing, and a lifetime's worth of spending habits. We have seen numerous couples in our practice who, prior to our bringing this up, had *no* idea about a previous bankruptcy, credit-score disaster, or looming financial trouble facing their partner. That's why we believe every couple should run and review their credit score and history together—not just as a financial matter, but as an indicator of lifestyle and personal discipline.

Money fights can be the number-one killer of marriages. A lot of people talk about sexual issues as the "big" thing, but in our offices, that's not the top concern that brings people in. Put it this way. After a few years (or maybe even a few months), it's unlikely that you'll have sex every day, but you *will* spend money every day. And not just once a day, but all day long. Issues of disagreement in this area will therefore become *repeated* points of stress. Regardless of income or socioeconomic status, finances are typically the number-one stress most husbands and wives face when their marriage is in trouble and they seek professional assistance. It's essential for couples to consider the potential impact of money on their overall marital satisfaction. If handled wisely, money can serve you; if handled poorly, or if not handled at all, it can drive many couples apart.

Depending upon your background and experiences, you will have different opinions about money and finances. For instance, if your parents were both conservative with money, you may be also, but that doesn't mean this is true for your soon-to-be spouse. He or she may have come from a family where money wasn't a priority, or the budget was rarely in balance, or giving was perceived as more virtuous than saving. Different ideas about money may seem cute during courtship, but we can assure you they will quickly become an area of conflict between the two of you once you settle into real life as a married couple. If you don't get on the same page in this area, you're going to have a very rocky relationship.

What we're about to say might sound unspiritual to some of you, but the reality is that getting married is similar to establishing a business in many respects, and wise couples treat it as such. You are going to have to produce income, manage income, and pay off debt. Successful couples will therefore treat family finances with the same level of scrutiny that a business does. Christians can get sloppy here, using a false understanding of "dependence on God" as an excuse to cut corners or not even consider basic financial practices. Discussing these issues ahead of time can spare you much misery in the future and give you tremendous peace in the present.

There are three basic questions the two of you should analyze and discuss at this point in your journey together:

1. How will you make money?

2. How will you spend (and give) money?

3. How will you save money?

This is also the time when you can decide who will work—one or both of you. Will this always be true, or will you change that plan when you have children? While you can't predict the future, you can have essential conversations about the values that will inform all future decisions. You can also begin praying together for the Lord's guidance in these money matters. Think about it: if you get on the same page here, you've just removed the number-one reason couples get into arguments. This is a talk worth having!

1. How did your family handle money when you were growing up? For example, did your parents operate on a budget? Was money or the lack thereof a source of stress? As a child, did you have to save up to buy something you wanted, or were you given most things? Go into even more detail here. Questions can't elicit everything that needs to be discussed with such diverse histories, so take some time to describe your personal history with money.

When you meet as a couple with your mentor, compare and contrast the ways your families handled money. Spend the first part of your session together talking out your personal histories.

2. How are you motivated by money? Does it cause you to work harder? Does it make you anxious? Does it make you feel more secure?

3. What positive role models have you had in terms of finances? In what ways were they role models?

4. Do you enjoy managing money (budgeting, investing, balancing bank accounts, making sure bills are paid)? Is this something you'd want to do, or would you prefer your spouse do it?

5. Once you get married, basic financial management will require certain tasks to be accomplished sooner rather than later. Assign the

following to one spouse, the other, or both, and give a date by when you intend to complete them:

a. Establish a simple will and/or trust with an attorney who can amend the legal paperwork as you grow your family.

b. Apply for (or update) life insurance, health insurance, disability insurance, or any other insurance needs you feel are warranted for your situation.

c. Combine your bank accounts, update retirement plans, and establish joint savings and investments.

d. Evaluate your charitable priorities to reflect the combining of your financial interests.

6. Do you believe in living by a budget, or would that feel too confining?

7. How do you plan to earn money? Will one person earn the bulk (or all) of the income? Will this change over time? What about when you have kids?

8. Do you believe in tithing at church and giving to charity? How important is that to you? Would there ever be a time when you would be angry if your spouse gave money away?

9. When it comes to investing, would you say you are an aggressive investor (putting capital at risk to get a bigger return), a moderate investor (moderate risk for a moderate return), or conservative investor (low risk for a lower return)?

10. If you're conservative, could you sleep at night if you knew your spouse was aggressive? If you're aggressive, how frustrated would you get if your spouse always wanted to keep extra savings in the bank and invest in bonds and T-bills?

11. How much should your future spouse be able to spend without talking to you about it?

12. Most financial advisors say couples should plan to spend no more than three or four years' salary on their house ($100,000 yearly income = $300,000 to $400,000 house). Are you the type who would prefer to buy a smaller house that might only cost one or two years' salary, or a larger house that might cost five or six years' salary, hoping to "grow into it"?

13. Is any kind of debt acceptable to you? If so, what kinds, and what percentage of your income?

14. What debt are you currently carrying: list mortgage payments, car loans and leases, school debt, credit card debt, etc.

15. Finally, what are your financial goals? To give away a certain amount? To retire by a certain age? To set up trust funds for grandchildren, or to earn enough to just get by while you enjoy all you can here on earth?

FINANCES

Remember this: Whoever sows sparingly will also reap sparingly, and whoever sows generously will also reap generously. Each … should give what he has decided in his heart to give, not reluctantly or under compulsion, for God loves a cheerful giver.

—2 Corinthians 9:6–7

When our oldest son and his wife were first engaged, we (Steve and Rebecca) gave them several books to read as part of their premarital journey. They willingly agreed and seemed to enjoy the process immensely. Then one evening they decided the two of us should take a quiz included in one of the resources so they could see how much we knew about each other. After almost thirty years, we were fairly confident we'd do okay, and we're happy to report we did better than okay—we got a perfect score. One question, however, was very revealing: it turns out we both happen to be givers rather than savers. When we were asked what we value most, both of us were in strong agreement—we get far more joy out of giving rather than saving.

By the way, this isn't necessarily something to brag about! We both love to give gifts—to one another, to our church and ministries, and to family and friends. As a consequence, we haven't always been the best stewards in regards to saving for ourselves. When we were first married, we often found ourselves over budget, trying to figure out where we had spent what we thought we had saved. Thankfully, our heavenly Father is gracious and merciful, and in 2 Corinthians 9:6–7, He encourages sharing in a happy, unselfish manner. God never gives grudgingly to us, so it's important we learn His spirit of generosity. The key, like most things in life, is finding the right balance. Both of you need to discover how to be giving while at the same time taking care of what God has given you.

This is a great moment in your lives to reconsider your resources and determine how you've been using them and how you will do so in the future. Perhaps you've been foolish with your money, spending more than you take in. Maybe you've been heroic at saving but realize you haven't given away much at all. Maybe you've never even thought about money and can't account for what you've been entrusted with.

Use this new season in your life as an opportunity to evaluate where you've been, where you're at now, and just as importantly, where you want to be next year, five years from now, and even on into retirement. Discussing your thoughts about saving versus sharing with others in your lives is important, especially earlier rather than later in your relationship. Talk about how you plan to budget and pay bills as well as how you'd like to spend your "fun money" so you can enjoy your life too. Finally, don't forget to decide how you plan to give back to God—with your treasure, time, and talents.

SPIRITUAL INTIMACY

We love because he first loved us.

—1 John 4:19

If you want to become the kind of spouse who truly loves, gives, serves, forgives, encourages, and supports, you're going to need some help. None of this comes naturally to any spiritually fallen human being. Marriage in particular isn't easy; in fact, it may well be the most difficult challenge you ever undertake. But in its difficulty, it can help you learn how to rely on God—that is, to first receive God's love and then pass that love on to others, beginning with your spouse. "We love because he *first* loved us." The missing ingredient in so many marriages that fail is the most important one—spiritual intimacy, learning how to draw near *to* God for His love and *upon* God for His resources in order to go the distance.

Most people don't enter marriage thinking, "I can't wait to surrender all of my wants, needs, hopes, and desires to another person—life is simply not going to be about me anymore!" Yet this is exactly what a sacred marriage is all about. The very essence of surrendering yourself involves sacrifice, and in marriage this must start with a willingness to give of yourself more than you want to get. You can do that only if you're connected to the God who gives without measure.

What all this means is that everything ultimately flows from this foundation of spiritual intimacy with God. The best worshippers are therefore usually the best spouses—those who have learned how to draw near to God and pour out His unending love to others. While the two of you may have different styles of worship or viewpoints about devotion, your joint goal is to glorify the Lord and work together as a team to please Him.

1. How important is it to you to regularly participate in corporate worship? More specifically, how often do you plan to go to church: every now and then, monthly, weekly, many times a week? Are you willing to compromise on this?

2. How important is it to you to be part of a small group or Bible study in addition to weekly worship gatherings?

3. Describe your personal devotional habits. Do you pray daily? How often do you read or study the Bible? What do you think about fasting and other spiritual disciplines? Do you expect to engage in these activities alone, with your mate, or in a combination of the two?

4. Do you desire to eventually have family devotions? If so, what will they look like? Who will lead them?

As we share with many couples, a developing and mature intimacy with Christ should include the following:

- Active corporate and individual worship
- Studying God's Word
- Peer/mentor relationships with same-gender friends for accountability and encouragement
- Actively using your spiritual gifts for the advancement of God's kingdom

While each of you is individually working on this personally focused intimacy with Christ, you must also begin developing your spiritual intimacy as a couple. We recommend that you begin with these steps:

- Have regular devotional times together (see Gary's *Devotions for a Sacred Marriage* and Rebecca's *New Beginnings* devotional).
- Worship together each week.
- Pray together daily.
- Fellowship with other peer and/or mentor couples.
- Utilize your spiritual gifts in practical ways together (volunteer at your church and/or in the community).

After decades of working with couples, we can confidently report to you that marital satisfaction is directly linked to spiritual intimacy, both with the Lord and with each other. When individuals are satisfied with God and His plan for their lives, they enjoy all that He has given them. People who are surrendered to the Lord are also more willing to surrender to others, understanding that serving their spouse is really an act of worship to God.

5. Do you agree that your long-term marital satisfaction is first connected to spiritual intimacy with your Creator? Why or why not?

6. Have you already begun building spiritual intimacy as a couple? How so? If not, should you take time to develop these patterns (individually and jointly) before moving forward in your

relationship? (Going into marriage without a strong spiritual base would be like going into a medieval battle without a coat of armor.)

7. Do you know of any good role models of spiritual intimacy? What lessons can you apply to your own lives from their example?

8. Do you have peers and mentors who can encourage your spiritual development? What plan do you have for developing and maintaining these relationships in the future?

9. At the end of your life, as the two of you look back on (hopefully) many decades of worship and service, how would you like people to describe your marriage?

"POWER" COUPLES

She speaks with wisdom,
  and faithful instruction is on her tongue.
She watches over the affairs of her household
  and does not eat the bread of idleness.
Her children arise and call her blessed;
  her husband also, and he praises her.
—Proverbs 31:26–28

The term *power couple* has been used for some time to describe a husband and wife who seem to have it all. In modern society, they're typically wealthy, smart, sophisticated, and strong influencers in the world. The media exalts politicians and lawyers or movie producers and actors, and these powerful people not only intrigue us but are also often highly esteemed. Sadly, these are usually also the couples that make other headlines because they've had any number of moral failures, embarrassing brushes with the law, or stints in rehab.

In Proverbs 31 we find a very different sort of husband and wife. They complement each other perfectly. The wife's influence is so powerful that her husband and family can't help but praise her. The spouse is equally worthy of admiration: "Her husband is respected at the city gate, where he takes his seat among the elders of the land" (v. 23). He meets with the leaders in order to give advice and help people solve their problems. His wife also provides wise instruction and is faithful in all of the roles and responsibilities God has given her.

What a terrific example this ancient couple is for modern-day marriages. Because of their godliness and earnest commitment to God and each other, their love is amplified. Men and women around them can't help but notice, and their relationship has truly stood the test of time.

They are, as a couple, what Isaiah prophesied of individuals in Isaiah 32:2–4:

Each … will be like a shelter from the wind
and a refuge from the storm,
like streams of water in the desert
and the shadow of a great rock in a thirsty
land.

Notice the power of these lives! A holy couple, joined in marriage, can be a spiritual force, a God-oasis in a world that desperately needs spiritually strong people. When the winds of turmoil hit, such people become shelters; their faith provides a refuge to all who seek shelter. By their words and actions, by the way they listen and the characters they have forged together, they are like refreshing streams of water in the desert, affirming what God values most. When the heat of temptation tears this world apart, godly couples become like the shadow of a great rock. These God-oases carry Christ to the hurting, to the ignorant, to those in crisis. They *will* be sought out—and they *will* have something to say.

Can you imagine this kind of spiritual connection in your own marriage? Do you long to have a partner who praises rather than speaks disrespectfully? Who joins you in reaching out to a hurting world, and who supports you when you falter? Who inspires you with their faith and courage, who covers you with their prayers, who encourages you with their tongue? Are you both striving to grow closer to God so you will not only glorify Him but also do great things for His kingdom (and for each other)? If you hope to attain this kind of relationship, then you've got to start by becoming the kind of deeply spiritual and committed partner you envision for today and all of your tomorrows. Remember, we love only because He first loved us. Let God love you as individuals, learn to love each other as spouses, and then be prepared to be used by God to spread that love to a needy and hurting world.

THE MARRIAGE MENTOR'S CONVERSATIONAL SESSION GUIDE

Whether you are a pastor, professional counselor, or marriage mentor to this couple, we thank you for helping these two individuals work their way through the premarital process. Below you will find suggestions for assisting them in delving deeper into the topics in each session, and we recommend that you hold them accountable to the guidelines listed in "For Couples: How to Use This Guide" found at the beginning of the book. We describe your involvement in the process as encouraging the couple to *scuba* versus *snorkel* in their relationship. We want the couple to take their conversations deeper than ever before, so don't be afraid to lead them to new levels of intimacy in these sacred conversations.

Please note that while this guide has been organized into nine sessions, we have not attached a time interval to define a session. Any of these nine sessions may take several meetings to thoroughly complete, depending upon the needs of each couple. In some cases, professional counseling will be needed to supplement the conversations recommended here in order for the couple to prepare for a successful and satisfying marriage.

SESSION 1: PRE-ENGAGEMENT PUNCH LIST

1. Either before or after your first meeting together, have each individual complete a Personal History Questionnaire (see Appendix B). You may explain that this is the type of questionnaire married couples are often asked to fill out when they see a professional counselor about problems in their marriage. You are asking them to answer these self-revealing questions now because we believe that a large percentage of couples can avoid professional counseling during their marriage if they address these questions beforehand. Now is the time for each individual to become aware of and begin to deal with his or her own history and that of the future mate. We strongly encourage couples not to skip or gloss lightly over any of the questions, because the ones they'd rather bypass usually are the areas that will cause them heartache later on.

2. Once they've completed the questionnaire, review it with them—first one-on-one with each individual and then with both of them together.

3. Ask the couple to discuss their strengths, weaknesses, and any concerns that arose from their own and their potential mate's Personal History Questionnaire results. If discussing the questionnaire takes a full meeting and you need to postpone the rest of session 1 for your next meeting, the time will be well spent.

If the questionnaire brings to light any issues that you feel you are not trained to address, consider referring one or both individuals to a professional counselor. In some cases you may want to encourage them not to plan a wedding until they have addressed these issues with a counselor, but in most cases you can reassure them that seeing a counselor does not brand them as unmarriageable. In fact, dealing with any problem areas will make them an even more desirable mate than before. The point of seeing a counselor now is to avoid the *necessity* of seeing one later after the commitment for marriage has been made.

4. Next, ask each individual to write an auto-biographical, up-to-date history paper of his or her personal story. Tell the couple that they'll have an opportunity to share this autobiography with each other and with you in your discussion of session 5, so they have several weeks to complete it. Explain also that they won't be *required*

to share anything they're not ready to share at that time, so they can be completely honest in this writing.

They must agree to leave *nothing* out. Anything left out of the autobiography probably is of most importance to the individual and the couple regarding their future marital satisfaction. Typically, this assignment should include about one double-spaced page per each year of life lived (a twenty-five-year-old should have a twenty-five-page paper because life has that many details worth sharing). This history should include things about their families, friends, experiences, and feelings throughout their lives thus far. It should begin with details about what an individual knows about the environment and circumstances that he or she was born into. The more detail, the better. Next, the real story begins with first memories and moves forward from there. That usually occurs for most of us at age three or four. Those who were reared in an abusive environment will have blackout periods at times through elementary school before their story picks up again.

We realize this sounds like a *tremendous* amount of work, and in one sense, it is. But remind the couple that the more they put into this, the more they will get out of it. And then ask them if they want a normal, average marriage, or if they want to begin taking steps to have an unusually intimate marriage.

SESSION 2: THE DOUBT-FREE WEDDING DAY

1. It's your role to ensure that these conversations include answers to all questions that are completely candid, without reservation, and satisfying to the couple and to you. Feel free to go deeper into any question you feel needs more consideration in order to alleviate any doubts about readiness for marriage.

2. Assist in identifying potential problems, and attach specific solutions to each unresolved issue. (Relational troubles do not get better over time. They typically get worse.)

3. Discuss specific conflict-resolution skills so that the couple will be prepared to deal with problems we can't cover in premarital conversations. (We will be discussing more thoughts on conflict resolution in session 6.)

4. If necessary, remind the couple that it is better to admit that an announced engagement was

premature or unwise and to call the wedding off than to go through with the wedding simply because it's been announced. This session is designed in part to give you, the counselor, the opportunity to question the wisdom of their choice, should the choice be unwise. They need to see that they are making a life commitment, and any embarrassment or pain will be minuscule in comparison to entering a problematic marriage.

SESSION 3: YOUR COVENANT MARRIAGE

1. Process the statistics for divorce today with the couple and how their day-to-day marital lives are predictors and directly correlated to their future marriage and family satisfaction and success. Few, if any, plan on getting a divorce, but their little daily actions will eventually lead to the big disappointment of bringing the marriage to an end.

2. Help the couple define the parameters of their marital vows.

3. Have the couple share about their current and future network of peers and mentors who can walk through life with them.

4. Discuss with the couple why seeking professional help may be needed one day with problems they may face—individually, as a couple, or with their family. Help them understand that successful couples never fear professional marital/family support.

5. If one partner seems open to divorce even after going through this session, point this out to the other partner, and question whether they think it is wise to enter marriage with someone who thinks there is a wide-open (or even partially open) back door.

6. Review good role models that the couple has in terms of covenant marriages. Discuss the positive attributes of those marriages, and then process how the couple can work to incorporate these characteristics into their own relationship.

SESSION 4: AND THE TWO SHALL BECOME ONE

1. Be on the lookout for evasion. If couples begin hiding from each other even before marriage, the future looks bleak in terms of the two of them building lasting intimacy. Whatever individuals are most uncomfortable sharing is where you need to

press them to share; those are the issues that guided premarital counseling is designed to address.

2. "Little" secrets often set the pattern for outright lying. Find out why one of the partners has any reluctance to share Internet, email, or social-media passwords. The willing partner might be reluctant to press this, so it's your job to be their advocate and explain that truly satisfying marital intimacy comes from having an "all in" attitude.

3. If one of the partners seems reluctant to share financial resources and insists on a prenuptial agreement for unwise reasons, make sure you explore what's really going on beneath the surface. "Planning to fail," i.e., planning to make getting a divorce as easy as possible, is a disastrous mind-set with which to begin a marriage.

4. Notice whether both partners seem capable of and willing to truly "leave" their families and cleave to each other. Also explore whether they are willing to adopt each other's family, as appropriate. It might help here if you bring up obvious but painful dynamics (a controlling mother-in-law or father-in-law, an abusive parent, etc.) and discuss strategies to navigate these relationships accordingly.

SESSION 5: BUILDING A FAMILY

1. Refer back to the couple's autobiographical stories from session 1 and discuss the couple's baggage, burdens, and blessings from their family of origin that will impact them as parents.

2. You might be surprised at how few couples talk through the financial implications of raising children. Some women assume they will stay home as soon as kids arrive, while their husbands expect them to keep working; other women plan to keep working and are seriously considering men who want their wives to stay home. Ask the honest questions: "So, if one of you plans to stay home, are you willing to live on the other's salary?" or, "And you feel comfortable, then, with having your children spend a significant amount of time in day care?"

3. If you notice that one partner seems particularly unsuited to be a parent, don't hesitate to point this out to the other partner if they are eager to have children. In our opinion, if someone truly wants to raise a family, they have no business marrying someone who is not suited to be the partnering parent. Help both members of the couple understand that getting married is, as we

stated, usually about building a family, not just creating a permanent couple.

4. Ask each individual to consider what their vision for their family is. The questions should raise the most pertinent issues—how many children, when, etc.

5. Process the difficulties and stresses related to noncompliant or disabled children.

SESSION 6: CONSTRUCTIVE CONFLICT

1. As a counselor or mentor, you know how certain conflict is, so you also know how vital it is for couples to go into marriage with the understanding that conflict is inevitable and that certain conflict-resolution skills are essential if the marriage is to survive. This is a session that might require a follow-up if the couple isn't getting it. Take the time to process with the couple what their history was like in terms of resolving—or not resolving—conflict. How will this affect their current and future life together?

2. Note that this session may require more informal teaching than the others. Few people grow up with mature conflict-resolution skills, so have

some resources handy if couples need outside study.

3. Assist the couple in coming up with non-negotiable principles by which they will resolve conflict. During marriage, couples often fight about the process of conflict resolution ("You shouldn't have talked to so-and-so about it....") as much as they do the original issue. Taking the time to set some basic ground rules will spare the couple many future arguments.

4. Every couple needs to develop a strategy through an objective third party when it comes to conflict when their own methods fail. Discuss what plan they will implement should such a situation arise. Specifically, who is their support system? *Name* the people, even ranking them in order of priority. This may sound like overkill to the couple, but your seriousness now will serve them in the future when conflict does arise.

5. Help the couple understand the process of forgiveness as part of conflict resolution in their relationship. The process should begin by forgiving all others in their lives. Gossip and grudges will never allow marital intimacy to fully develop and will in many cases destroy the marriage

altogether. Don't be afraid to be blunt: it is foolish to marry someone who is either unable or unwilling to forgive. If conflict is inevitable—as it is—the ability to let go of past hurt is vital.

SESSION 7: DEVELOPING AND MAINTAINING SEXUAL INTIMACY

1. You must take a thorough sexual history of each individual and then process this with them as a couple. You can reference the appropriate sections of the questionnaire for discussion points (Appendix B). Note our comments within the chapter about the level of detail appropriate for the marriage mentor versus the professional counselor. If you are not a trained therapist, don't delve into areas you're not qualified to treat. However, don't ignore them either, but recommend that the couple receive professional help.

2. It is at this point, pre-engagement or pre-marriage, that a couple must decide if they are going to exchange their sexual histories. It's our recommendation they begin their marital journey with no secrets and that each of them should be totally informed before committing to covenant marriage.

3. Help the couple develop and script a strategic action plan for developing and maintaining spiritual, emotional, and physical/sexual intimacy.

4. Some couples, particularly those with no prior sexual experience, may need assistance as to appropriate resources to study before the wedding day. If they grew up in a sexually repressive environment, they may need spiritual counsel to accept the holiness of marital sexuality.

5. We recommend that couples decide on what form of birth control they plan to use (if any) before they get married, along with the ethical issues involved. This is where pastoral counseling can be very helpful in guiding the couple to make a wise choice.

SESSION 8: MONEY, MONEY, MONEY

1. Some of the couples may think that sharing credit histories sounds extreme or makes them seem suspicious of each other. Assure them that it's wise for any couple to periodically review their credit report, even after marriage, and that doing so now is merely the first step in a lifelong journey of being a faithful steward of God's resources. If one partner hesitates,

support the other partner in asking that person to reconsider. There is no valid reason for someone to refuse to share their credit history with a potential spouse.

2. Finances are the number-one reason couples have conflict, so don't cut corners here. Explore thoroughly how their parents handled money, how they deal with money, and how they hope to balance money matters as a couple.

3. What does the couple's financial plan look like? Have them discuss this concept together—short- and long-term goals included.

4. Unpack the concept of how emotions are connected to money, and talk about why this is a potentially volatile area of conflict for couples.

5. Have the couple create a mock budget based on their income and then discuss whether they can realistically commit to such a budget (without, by the way, incurring massive amounts of debt for the wedding and/or honeymoon).

6. Ask the couple to develop a plan for what they will do if conflict over finances reaches an impasse.

SESSION 9: SPIRITUAL INTIMACY

1. Develop and script a specific plan for spiritual intimacy that this man and woman can practice on an individual level first. Then move toward working on committing to this plan as a couple.

2. If it becomes apparent that one or both of them isn't truly a believer, be prepared to invite them to a life of faith. If one or both of them aren't in a relationship with Christ, they can't build true spiritual intimacy as a couple.

3. Pay particular attention to the questions regarding corporate worship attendance. Press for a commitment. We've seen far too many individuals act as if they *intend* to make church a priority, but after the wedding they choose not to.

4. Be prepared to discuss the problems of faith conflict: a Roman Catholic marrying a Baptist, a Pentecostal marrying a Presbyterian, etc. It's not enough to decide where they're going to get married; it's just as important to know where they plan to worship every week after that. In the flush of infatuation, couples often minimize the challenges these combinations represent. Sadly, the end result is that the family rarely worships together. If the

couple can't decide where they will attend church (and how often) before they get married, that's a huge red flag that perhaps they haven't thought through these issues in anywhere near acceptable specificity.

5. Ask the couple what current role models they would surround themselves with who will encourage their spiritual walk with the Lord.

6. Talk about whom the couple will be accountable to for support in their spiritual development.

PERSONAL HISTORY QUESTIONNAIRE

The following questionnaire is the one that has been used by Dr. Steve Wilke over the past twenty-five years for every person who has visited his office. We're including it here so you can see the depth of information that is required to help a couple consider such a momentous decision as entering marriage. You may choose not to use every question in your own particular setting. Dr. Wilke's rationale for these questions is revealed in the following, which is given to each person prior to receiving the questionnaire:

I am giving you this questionnaire for three important reasons. First, we have given this to every patient who has asked for our help. This is not unique to you or the reason you have come to ask for our help. Taking the time to write these answers down is probably not something you have ever done or will do again. It is important for you to look at yourself in such a way that respects the potential variables that impact you, the way you live your life, and those around you. Also, this will give me information that I need in order to rule out certain parts of your life and to know where we should focus our effort together. Every one of these questions has a specific purpose to improve you. If any of these questions are too personal and/or you do not feel comfortable answering them, pass them by. If I believe that they need to be addressed, I will ask you about them. You can opt not to answer, and I will move forward. I want you to understand the purpose of this exercise and be informed so that you can be as comfortable as possible in participating in making this counseling/ mentoring relationship as productive as possible. Any questions?

COUNSELING QUESTIONNAIRE

CONFIDENTIAL DATA INVENTORY

Purpose of this questionnaire: this questionnaire is designed to obtain a comprehensive picture of your background. By completing these questions as fully and accurately as you can, you will facilitate your therapeutic program. This questionnaire will save you both time and expense. You are requested to answer these routine questions on your own time rather than your actual counseling hour.

It is understandable that you might be concerned about what happens to this information about you. Case records are strictly confidential, and no one other than you and your therapist will be permitted to see the information.

NOTE: If you do not wish to answer any question, merely write "Do not care to answer."

I. GENERAL INFORMATION

Name: _____ Date: _____

Address: _____ Home phone: _____

City/State/Zip _____ Work phone: _____

Gender: _____ Age: _____ Date of birth:_____

Referred by: _____

Family doctor: _____

Please state your reasons for coming here for help. _____

_____

_____

How long have the above problems been concerning you? _____

_____

II. INDIVIDUAL HISTORY

Where were you born? _____

Were you a planned child? _____

Were you adopted? _____

If yes, please describe the circumstances:

When _____ Where _____

By whom _____ At what age _____

Did you or your mother have any complications during pregnancy or delivery? If so, describe. _____

_____

List all *serious* diseases or illnesses you had as a child. Include your age at the time: _____

_____

List all *serious* operations or accidents you had as a child. Include your age at the time of the illness: _____

_____

_____

Please describe any fearful or traumatic experiences not previously mentioned (deaths, moves, divorce, abuse, etc.): _____

_____

_____

Describe your earliest memory._____

_____

_____

At what age did you have problems with:

Eating _____ Sitting _____ Breathing _____ Toilet training _____
Walking _____ Talking _____ Rashes _____ Going to school _____

Did you have any of the following problems as an adolescent?

Bed-wetting _____ Hurting others ___ Fights _____ Hurting self _____
Lying _____ Accident-prone _____ Few friends _____ Stealing _____
Messing pants (BM) ___ Fire setting _____ Cheating _____ Fears_____
Breaking things _____ Nightmares _____ Sleepwalking _____
Thumb sucking _____ Stammering/stuttering _____ Tantrums _____

Were you raised by both parents? YES _____ NO _____
If no, by whom? _____

How much did your parents fight? _____

What type of fighting was involved? _____
_____

III. FAMILY HISTORY

Has or does a member of your family suffer(ed) from a mental dis-
turbance? YES _____ NO _____
If yes, what is the nature of the illness? _____
If yes, has it resulted in hospitalization/treatment? _____

How many brothers and sisters do you have? (Please provide ages and
names.)_____
_____
_____

Among the members of your family listed earlier:
I feel closest to _____
I feel least close to _____

How do you describe your own environment? _____
_____

Were/are you able to confide in your parents? YES _____ NO _____

Did your parents divorce or separate? YES _____ NO _____

If yes, how old were you? What were the circumstances and how did you react? _____
_____

Why did the divorce occur? _____
_____

With which parent did you live? _____

Did either parent remarry? (How old were you?) _____

Mark an F and an M on each line at the appropriate point that most closely describes your feelings regarding your father (F) and mother (M).

	1	2	3	4	5	
Strong						Weak
Warm						Cold
Close						Distant
Happy						Sad
Good						Bad
Interested						Disinterested
Smart						Stupid
Loving						Hateful
Masculine						Feminine

Industrious						Lazy
Generous						Stingy
Healthy						Sick
Accepting						Critical
Strict						Lax
Rich						Poor

My parents were: Excellent___ Good ___ Okay ___
Poor ___ Very poor ___

I was closest to: Mother ___ Father ___ Same ___ Neither ___

My parents were: Very strict ___ Strict ___ Moderate ___ Lenient ___

Compared to my brothers and sisters, my parents punished me:
More ___ Less ___ Same ___

IV. EDUCATIONAL HISTORY

What is the highest grade you completed? ___

What age did you begin school? ___

Were you kept behind or did you advance a grade? ___

Were you ever in any special classes? ___ Often truant? ___

Did you have any special difficulties or problems in school? YES ___ NO ___

If yes, please explain: _____

Did you have disciplinary problems? ___

What grades did you usually receive? ___

Did you enjoy school? ___

V. SCHOOL PARTICIPATION

How did you spend your leisure/free time?_____
_____

Were you involved in school activities?

Athletics: Active ___ Average ___ Some ___ None ___
Clubs: Active ___ Average ___ Some ___ None ___

Popularity? Very popular ___ Popular ___ Average ___
Unpopular ___ Very unpopular ___ Loner ___

Dating? Very much ___ Much ___ Average ___ Little ___
Very little ___ None ___

Age of first date? ___

VI. OCCUPATIONAL HISTORY

Number of jobs in the past 10 years: ＿＿

Have you ever been fired? Explain: ＿＿＿＿＿＿＿＿＿＿＿＿
＿＿＿＿＿＿＿＿＿＿＿＿＿＿＿＿＿＿＿＿＿＿＿＿＿＿＿＿＿＿＿

What job have you held the longest and for how long? ＿＿＿＿＿＿
＿＿＿＿＿＿＿＿＿＿＿＿＿＿＿＿＿＿＿＿＿＿＿＿＿＿＿＿＿＿＿

Number of promotions in the last years? ＿＿

Do you like being promoted? ＿＿

Are you satisfied with your current job? ＿＿ If not, please explain:
＿＿＿＿＿＿＿＿＿＿＿＿＿＿＿＿＿＿＿＿＿＿＿＿＿＿＿＿＿＿＿
＿＿＿＿＿＿＿＿＿＿＿＿＿＿＿＿＿＿＿＿＿＿＿＿＿＿＿＿＿＿＿

VII. GENERAL SEXUAL HISTORY

What were your parents' attitudes toward sex? ＿＿＿＿＿＿＿＿
＿＿＿＿＿＿＿＿＿＿＿＿＿＿＿＿＿＿＿＿＿＿＿＿＿＿＿＿＿＿＿

Was there sex instruction or discussion at home? ＿＿＿＿＿＿＿

How often did you masturbate as a child or teen? ＿＿＿＿＿＿

When do you currently masturbate? ＿＿＿＿＿＿＿＿＿＿＿＿＿

Does it bother you? _____

When and how did you learn about sex? _____

Are you or have you been sexually active outside of marriage? ____

Have you ever had a homosexual experience? ___

Have you ever been molested/abused/raped? ___

If yes, age at onset: ___

Have you ever had an unusual, unpleasant, or frightening sexual experience? _____

If yes, explain: _____
_____

In my opinion, sex is _____

Are you satisfied with your current spouse or lover? Explain: _____
_____

VIII. SEXUAL HISTORY FOR WOMEN ONLY

Age at onset of periods: ___ Were you prepared? ___

Do you experience any menstrual pain or irregularity? ___

Do your periods affect you emotionally? ____

Have you been treated for PMS? ____

Have there been any complications from pregnancies? ____

Have you ever had a miscarriage? ____ If yes, what and when was your emotional reaction? _____

Have you ever had an abortion? ____ If yes, what and when was your emotional reaction? _____

Have you or are you about to experience menopause? ____

IX. MARITAL HISTORY

Marital status: ____ Date of marriage: _____

How long did you know your spouse prior to marriage? _____ _____

Did you engage in premarital sex? ____

Were you pregnant at the time of marriage? ____

Is your sex life with your partner satisfactory? ____

Have you been married previously? ____

If yes, when and how long were you married? How did it end? ____
_____

Have there ever been any threats of violence from your spouse? ____
If yes, explain: _____

How are conflicts handled in your marriage? _____
_____

How did your parents handle marital conflicts? _____
Do you have any problems with marital communication? _____
_____

How is love and caring displayed in your marriage? _____
_____

How was love and caring displayed in your parents' marriage? ____
_____

Are you satisfied with your marriage? ____ If not, explain and state
how it might be improved: _____
_____

How many children do you have? ____
List the names and ages of all children and where they currently live:
_____
_____

X. MEDICAL HISTORY

List all current medications and reason for taking: _____
_____
_____

Are there any hereditary diseases in your family? _____

Have you ever had any sexually transmitted diseases? _____

List past psychiatric treatments or hospitalizations: _____
_____

Have you ever taken medication for emotional problems? ____ If yes,
please provide the type, dosage, when, and for how long: _____
_____
_____

Have you ever had suicidal thoughts? ____ Attempts? ____

Height:_____ Weight: _____

Are you satisfied with your appearance? ____

Do you have any physical handicaps? ____

How is your vision? _____

Please list any allergies: _____

How is your hearing? _____

Who is your family physician? _____

When was your last physical checkup? _____

List all hospitalizations: _____
_____
_____

Have you ever had problems with:
Compulsive eating? ____
Nervous eating? ____
Inability to eat? ____

Have you ever had seizures? YES ____ NO ____

Have you ever been unconscious? YES ____ NO ____

List all street drugs you have used: _____
_____

List all street drugs that you are currently using: _____
_____

Do you smoke? If yes, how much per day? _____

XI. MILITARY INFORMATION

Have you ever been in the military? _____

What branch? _____ What rank? _____

Type of discharge? _____

Did you serve in Vietnam or any other war? _____

XII. LEGAL

Have you ever been arrested? YES____ NO ____

Give reasons if yes: _____

_____

Have you ever been in jail? ____ If yes, please state the reason: ____

_____

Have you ever received a ticket for driving under the influence of drugs and/or alcohol? ____

XIII. PSYCHIATRIC BACKGROUND

List all psychiatric medications you have ever taken _____

_____

Have you ever received counseling before? YES ____ NO ____

If yes, where, when, and for what reasons? _____

_____

Has anyone in your family received counseling or been hospitalized for mental, emotional, or behavioral problems? YES ___ NO ___
If yes, who and for what reasons? _____
_____
_____
_____

XIV. SPIRITUAL ASSESSMENT (OPTIONAL)

What church, if any, were you raised in? _____
What church, if any, are you currently involved in? _____
How frequently do you attend church? _____
What church activities are you involved in? _____
_____

Do you read your Bible for:
Support ____ Guidance ____
Comfort ____ Knowledge ____
Other _____

Do you have a regular prayer life? YES ___ NO ___
Does your family pray together? YES ___ NO ___

Are you involved in any support/development groups? _____

Is there anyone that you are spiritually accountable to? YES ___
NO ___

What is the most positive aspect of your relationship with the Lord?

_____

_____

What area in your relationship with the Lord would you like to improve? _____

_____

Have there been any recent significant changes in your spiritual beliefs and type of worship? _____

_____

_____

Have you had a "born again" experience? ____

Describe your impression of who Jesus Christ is and what His personality might be like: _____

_____

_____

Do you have many friends? ____
1 ____ 2–3 ____ 4–6 ____ 6–10 ____ More ____

Do you enjoy being with people? YES ____ NO ____

Do you make friends easily? YES ____ NO ____

Do you have problems keeping friends? YES ____ NO ____

Do you prefer to be in large groups, small groups, or with only one other person?

_____

_____

Would you consider yourself a follower or a leader? ____

Who do you turn to when you have needs? _____

_____

_____

What are your good points and strengths? _____

_____

_____

What are your weaknesses? _____

_____

CHECKLIST QUESTIONS

	YES	NO
Has drinking ever interfered with work, school, or home life?		
Have you ever been in trouble with the law as a result of drinking?		
Have drugs ever caused trouble in your life?		

Have you ever been in trouble with the law because of drug use?		
Have you ever tried to commit suicide?		
Have you ever *thought* of committing suicide?		
Have you ever hurt someone physically so they needed medical attention?		
Have you ever been accused of hurting a child?		
Have you ever been accused of neglecting your child?		
Have you ever vomited in order to maintain your weight?		
Have you ever lost so much weight that others were concerned?		
Do you ever feel like hurting others?		
Were you hyperactive as a child?		
Are you sensitive or easily hurt?		
Do you often feel guilty?		
Are you a perfectionist?		
Do you have difficulty showing love and affection?		
Do you have difficulty receiving love and affection?		
Do you find yourself getting into trouble often?		

Have you been involved in a physical fight within the last six months?		
Do you have nightmares?		
Have you ever been physically, sexually, or emotionally abused by a spouse or a lover?		
Were you physically abused as a child?		
Were you sexually abused as a child?		
Were you neglected as a child?		
Have you ever been raped or had sexual contact against your will?		

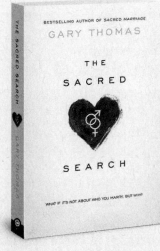

THE DVD STUDY RESOURCE FOR
THE SACRED SEARCH

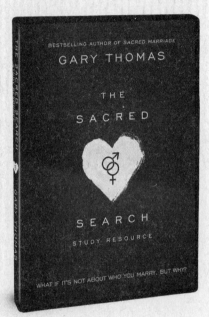

In this dynamic companion to the book, Gary will help singles move on from the idea of finding a "soul mate" and adopt the more biblical idea of finding their "sole mate," as they seek to dedicate their future marriages to God. This DVD also includes study questions designed to facilitate group discussion, interaction, and practical application.